California
in the War for Southern Independence

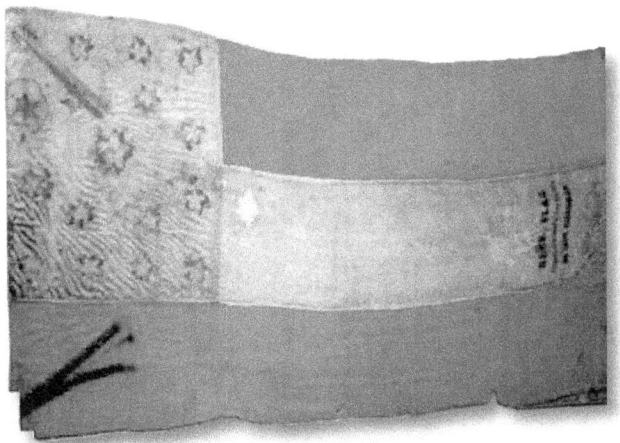

Laurence F. Talbott, PhD

Professor Emeritus,
California Polytechnic State University,
San Luis Obispo.

With illustrations and maps.

Deo Vindice.

REPRINTED BY

Wake Forest, NC
www.scuppernongpress.com

California In The War For Southern Independence
Laurence Fletcher Talbott, PhD

Copyright © 2024

Second Printing

The Scuppernong Press
PO Box 1724
Wake Forest, NC 27588
www.scuppernongpress.com

Cover and book design by Frank B. Powell, III

All rights reserved

Printed in the United States of America

No part of this book may be reproduced or transmitted in any form or by any means, electronic or mechanical, including photocopying, recording, or by any information and storage and retrieval system, without written permission from the editor and/or publisher.

International Standard Book Number ISBN 978-1-942806-69-1

Library of Congress Control Number: 2024946138

NOTE ON SPELLING AND STYLE.
From the Publisher

Some readers may be startled to find what may seem to them to be British spelling and style in a book printed in the United States of America; on closer inspection, however, and by comparison with American works printed in the nineteenth century and before, they will find there is very little difference in the spelling and style of educated British and American writers of the time.

Apart from pure reprints of later works and works of other publishers which they sell, the publishers of this and other original works hope to produce, as perfectly as possible, the tone, style, and spelling of the best writers of the period of which the books treat.

Since the time of Shakespeare, when the spelling and style of the English language became standard, there has been a difference in the spelling of certain words, exercised at the whim of the author and printer: apart from a few obscurities, these variant spellings occur in words which end in *-our* or *-or*, and in *-ise* and *-ize*. The best writers knew most of these *-our* words, almost all of them originally Latin, came into English through the intermediation of French, and thus have preferred the termination in *-our*, as in *honour*, which is more historically correct than *honor*; the *-ise* words, originally Greek, passed through Latin into French, which gave them to many other languages, including English, with the *-ise* spelling: *-ize* is etymologically incorrect, although used.

Neither of these variants was exclusively British or exclusively American: the *-ize* form of *-ise* gained the ascendancy in the seventeenth century, only to be eclipsed by the correct *-ise* in the eighteenth and later centuries. The *-our* spelling, used by Shakespeare and the great authors of the seventeenth century, was employed by all of the prominent writers of the eighteenth century, including George Washington; Benjamin Franklin, and Thomas Jefferson. *Waggon*, not *wagon*, is as American as anything, and was so spelled on both sides of the Atlantic, until, at the end of the eighteenth century, the crank Noah Webster, as may be seen in a letter of his to Thomas Jefferson now preserved at the Huntington Library, expressed his desire to mutate the entire English language, as a step towards which he wrote his dictionary the copies of which found so little favour in America they rotted in a storeroom. The popular dictionaries in America and England until the late nineteenth century were Dr. Johnson's and Walker's.

Dickens, nonetheless, writing in the 1840s, employed *-or*, whilst Abraham Lincoln used either *-our* or *-or*, and Robert E. Lee always wrote *-our*.

In the 1880s, the Merriam Company, with their army of door-to-door "drummers" or salesmen of books, seeking a way to make a good deal more money, bought the rights to Webster's Dictionary for a pittance, and produced a sumptuous edition of it which they sold door-to-door; in addition, the Merriam Company bribed educational officials, and so forced Webster's Dictionary on the unsuspecting poor of America, although their dictionary was made doubly obsolete before 1900 by the publication of the masterful Oxford Dictionary, a principal contributor to which was a shell-shocked Union officer who bad accidentally murdered a man on a trip to England, and wrote from his lifetime cell at Dartmoor Prison.

Before the Great War of 1914-1918, there was still little difference between American and British spelling in general, but, because of Prussian fomenting of anti-British feeling in the United States before her entry into that war in 1917, Webster's Dictionary was universally introduced into schools as the battering-ram of the Prussianised system of education, and the official and artificial division of English into American and British was created.

Centre, and many *-re* words, held ground firmly in many parts of America until their temporary defeat by the *center* and *-er* spellings at the time of the Second World War. The ligatures *-æ* and *-œ* were likewise gradually eliminated, so that many words became mispronounced, a tendency which flowed into Britain in the 1970s; Americans have begun, however, to reverse this bad trend, and so such words as *orthopædic* have correctly replaced the transient *orthopedic*, a spelling favoured between 1920 and 1970.

The English language has been wrecked by one hundred years of financial manipulation, and so, not only in the interest of providing a proper period flavour, but also in response to the growing demand on both sides of the Atlantic for the rescue of the English language from the jaws of ignorant mediocrity the publishers, with the agreement of the author of each title, are pleased to offer the rescue in the tangible form of the books which they publish, of which this is one.

       HALE & CO.
       Publishers. 1996

To
Joshua Frederick Cockey Talbott
Private, Company F, Second Maryland Cavalry, C. S. A

This work is affectionately dedicated
By The Author.

I have not yet had cause to regret the course I marked out at the commencement of this long, bloody, and desolating war. I am proud to fight, and, if necessary, die with a people who have contended so gallantly for their liberties against such fearful odds ... we feel it would be much better that the last man should perish in defence of his rights, rather than live as despised serfs of a northern despot. ... I have not heard a word from my people since I left California.
— Dan Showalter, (born in Pennsylvania), former California State Legislator, and afterwards lieutenant colonel, 4th Texas-Arizona Regiment, CSA
Official Records Series I. Vol. L. Pt. 2. pp. 1077-1078.

We might as well live in the Southern Confederacy as in Southern California.

San Francisco Bulletin. 1863.

THE CONTENTS.

Acknowledgments vii
Preface ix
Introduction xi
Chapter I. California in 1860, A Microcosm of America 1
Chapter II. Albert Sidney Johnston 11
Chapter III. Joseph Lancaster Brent... 29
Chapter IV. Cameron Erskine Thom 39
Chapter V. Judges David S. Terry, and Langsford W. Hastings 43
Chapter VI. The irrepressible Dan Showalter................................. 57
Chapter VII. The Resistance in Restive California 69
Chapter VIII. The Liberating Army That Did Not Come 99
Chapter IX. The Privateers 111
Chapter X. Partisan Rangers... 119
Chapter XI. Guerrillas. 135
Chapter XII. Epilogue 153
Index of Names 157

List of Illustrations.

1. The State Split of 1860.. xvi
2. Albert Sidney Johnston 12
3. Map of The Itinerary taken by A. S. Johnston's party
   from California to Texas... 13
4. The Muster Roll of the Los Angeles Mounted Rifles
   in early 1861 20
5. The Johnston Party Crossing The Desert 24
6. News of the arrival of the Californians at Mesilla....................... 28
7. Southern California bordering on the Confederate States 70
8. The *Fresno Times*, resurrected from the ruins
   of the *Equal Rights Expositor* 84
9. The Division of New Mexico Territory In 1861 98
10. News of the War as Related by the *Mesilla Times* in 1861....... 103
11. The Battle of Valverde... 134

Laurence F. Talbott, PhD

ACKNOWLEDGMENTS.

It would be unfortunate indeed if I did not acknowledge the support received since my entry into a field on which little previous attention had been bestowed; the research for this effort, therefore, required extensive use of libraries. The guidance and cooperation of the courteous and expert staffs of the following libraries in California is gratefully acknowledged:.

California State Library and Archive, Sacramento; California Historical Society, San Francisco; City of Los Angeles Public Library; Placer County Library, Auburn; Eldorado County Library, Placerville; Amador County Library, Jackson; Community Memorial Museum of Sutter County; Searld Library, Nevada City; Stockton Public Library; Vacaville Public Library; El Monte Historical Museum; Beal Memorial Library, Bakersfield; Holt Atherton Library, University of the Pacific, Stockton; Colusa County Library; Nevada County Library, Nevada City; Fresno County Public Library; Mendocino County Historical Society, Ukiah; Tulare County Free Library System; The California State Polytechnic University Robert F. Kennedy Interlibrary Loan System.

The curator of the California State Capitol Museum at Sacramento, Mr. Vito Sgromo, provided the beautiful photograph of the uniquely Californian "Biderman" Confederate flag (on the cover), together with its story from the *Sacramento Union,* a very valuable contribution received with much· appreciation.

Mr. Dick Marquette, the local historian of Marysville, made possible my unlimited use of the California Room of the Marysville Library, and provided much information from the *California Express,* as well as about the Thom family. Mr. John Swisher, of the Council of California Historical Societies, was generous with much obscure, but useful, history. Mr. Charles R. Heil, of Ventura, supplied leads to the fascinating interplay between the old Califomio families and the Confederacy through their friend, Joseph Lancaster Brent. Mr. William Harland Boyd, a prominent historian of the Kern County Historical Society, led me to the primary sources that affirmed the actions of Californian Confederate guerrillas in the Central Valley and region of Ft. Tejon. Mrs. Jane Johansson, of Prior, Oklahoma, was kind enough to send me the particulars of the service of Joseph Lancaster Brent as a Confederate general in the Red River Campaign. Mr. Barron Smith, of the California Division of the Sons of Confederate Veterans, was a steady source of leads to valuable information. Mr. Gene Armistead, author and historian, shared his treasury of knowledge

Laurence F. Talbott, PhD

of the Los Angeles Mounted Rifles, and of that organization's contributions to the Southern cause. The Swedish author, Herr Bertil Haggman, of the European Camp of the Sons of Confederate Veterans, and probably the world's authority on Confederate partisan warfare, generously provided his expertise in the legal standing of partisan ranger and guerrilla commands. Mr. Robert J. Chandler, Historian for Wells Fargo Bank at San Francisco, gave me the benefit of his keen insight into the editorial policies of Californian newspapers of the time, and the consequences of those policies.

Words are inadequate to express my appreciation for the assistance given to me by my wife, Patsy Anne Talbott; it does not go beyond saying that, without her, this book would not have been written. Her hours of searching through microfilms and microfiches, sometimes on very ailing equipment, the notes from these which she made when there was no printer attached to the viewing machinery, her persistence in pursuing murky leads long after I was ready to abandon them, and her long hours of work in typewriting, proofreading, and rewriting material which had sunk into the unexplored depths of the computer, is infinitely more than any reasonable person might expect: to her, my gratitude is boundless.

To Edwin Hale, Esq., the founder of the *Monthly Gazette of Historical Events* and Hale & Co., publishers, for suggesting that we serialize part of the book in the *Monthly Gazette*, and then agreeing to edit this book, and bring it to the light of day in so authentic a garb, I tender my right hearty thanks, . which he requests ought to be shared by my daughter, Mary Anne Talbott, Design Editor for the *Contra Costa Times*, for her timely assistance to him in the preparation of the galleys.

To all of the mentioned and the unmentioned I offer my most sincere and humble thanks.

Laurence Fletcher Talbott
San Luis Obispo, California
November 17, 1998

PREFACE.

On July 4, 1861, at Sacramento, California, Major J. P. Gillis decided to celebrate not only America's independence from Britain, but that of the South from the North. At about 10 P. M, after an exhibition of fireworks, he unfurled a Confederate flag which had been wrapped about his walking stick, and marched up and down the boardwalk before the St. George Hotel at the corner of 4th and J. Streets; most of those present appeared to be Southern sympathizers, pleased with the display of the flag.

Not all of those viewing this scene approved of it, however: J. W. Biderman and Curtis Clark watched with anger. After Major Gillis had demonstrated his feelings, Biderman and Clark followed him; Biderman approached Gillis, caught him by the throat with his left hand, and, with his right, tore the flag from the stick, and put it in his pocket. The account of the incident in the *Sacramento Daily Union* did not reveal the relative sizes or ages of the two antagonists; the Major was apparently a fighter, and called out to the crowd for a knife, but, no one proffering a weapon, Biderman's assault was successful. He cried out that "no such flag as that could be carried in this town" in his presence, and left the scene, taking the flag with him.

Biderman subsequently brought a large number of friends to the St. George; two of these friends, Frank Burns and A. Rhodes, waved the flag, and invited any "secessionists" to come and take it. No one tried. Major Gillis later "earnestly plead for the flag's return," but to no avail. The flag was considered by those who had it in their possession to be "too valuable a trophy to surrender … voluntarily."

The history of the flag does not continue until some time later. There seems to be no record of how or when, but the flag became the property of the California State Capitol Museum. The flag is made of silk, and is a variant of the First National Flag, the Stars and Bars, of the Confederacy. The difference is, that, in place of the original seven stars in the canton, there are seventeen white five-pointed stars. Inscribed on the white bar in the middle is "Rebel Flag. Captured July 4, 1861. By Jack Biderman." The display at the museum states this is "the only known Confederate flag captured in California during the Civil War." It is truly a Californian flag, of unique design. Designated "The Biderman Flag," it might better be named for Major J. P. Gillis, its owner.

The incident which occurred on the streets of California's capital city on July 4, 1861, and the flag that brought it about, are prophetic and

Laurence F. Talbott, PhD

symbolic of the secessionist movement in the state: open advocation and defence of the cause, defeat by a more powerful adversary, and all of this forgotten by history with only a battered *memento* remaining.[1]

1. California State Capitol Museum, Sacramento. State Capitol Room B-27.

INTRODUCTION.

The history of California during the American War Between the States has usually been written with little attention to the war's impact on the lives of Californians or the sectional struggles within the state.[1]

Hubert Howe Bancroft, the compiler of Californian history, describes commitment and physical risk-taking in behalf of the Confederacy, mostly in footnotes, with no interpretation of the importance of those actions:[2] other authors follow a similar pattern. Some books have been published, many of them privately, recounting the history of individual communities which may or may not have anything at all to say about the local attitude towards the War, or what happened there as a result of the war; there are community historical publications telling of prominent California citizens who served the South, which service is left unmentioned in their standard biographies. There is often useful information in community histories, but in the form of disconnected bits and pieces.

Books featuring the War in the Far West have been mainly concerned with the manner in which the Union forces dealt with the Confederate campaign in New Mexico Territory and the seceded Confederate Arizona Territory within her boundaries; there is little discussion of California, although California is usually acknowledged as a Confederate objective.[3]

Some of the best sources of published information regarding support for the Confederacy from within California are historical journals; many contributors to such journals have done extensive archival research into specific, fascinating events, but stay within the bounds of the topic that they address, having no regard for its implications. In general, these historians describe events from the Northern point of view, and provide little or no particulars concerning the opponents; the Californian secessionist is characterized as a nuisance which must be dealt with from time to time.

The best information about Californian secessionists may be obtained from original documents to be found in the public libraries of the local communities of California, the archives and library of the State of California, newspapers of the period, and the U. S. Government's publication, *The War of the Rebellion: A Compilation of the Official Records of the Union and Confederate Armies*, Series 1, Volume IV, and Series I, Volume L, Parts 1 and 2.

All of the above, although they do not· make plain the struggle of the secessionists of California to bring the state into the Confederacy, do contain important pieces, and, when put together, the pieces indicate that an

Laurence F. Talbott, PhD

important part of Californian history has not been written; this historical vacuum was predicted by Elijah R. Kennedy in his book, *The Contest for California in 1861*, published in 1912.

Kennedy writes of "the perilous state of affairs on the Pacific Slope," stating: "It will be interesting to note how little the 'history books' have to say on the subject, and how incorrect much of it is." He continues with a discussion of then contemporary historians, including: Von Holst, who, he believes, does not comprehend the movement for secession; George Ticknor Curtis, whose work is said to contain nothing of the movement for secession in California; the publication, *American History Told by Contemporaries*, which has not a word; Woodrow Wilson, in his *History of the American People*, who is oblivious of any relation of the Pacific states to the War; and Horace Greeley's *History of the American Conflict*, which makes no mention of California.

Kennedy gives examples of the works of several other historians, including *The History of the United States* by James Schoulder, who penned such lines as "the Pacific Coast state of California ... so utterly beyond the range of military operations that filial love furnished the only pledge of abiding loyalty to the Union. ... " Kennedy says further,

Hubert Howe Bancroft's *History of the Pacific States* is recognized as an invaluable compilation. Some of the volumes devoted to California contain many facts relating to the secession movement, many, though by no means all or nearly all; but they are so distributed, and so associated with various contexts, as to be deprived of their convincingness ... many of them are relegated to the unsuitable obscurity of footnotes."[4]

Kennedy was a colonel in the Union Army, whose book was written to give credit to Colonel E. D. Baker for saving California for the Union; in the process of compiling it, however, he recognized indirectly the strength and dedication of those Californians who tried to move the state, all or part, into the Confederacy. His work has been criticized by several historians who believe no one saved California for the Union, and that she was a strongly Union state that did not need saving.[5]

Until the history of the efforts of California's people who I believed in the righteousness of the Southern cause is understood, a comprehensive knowledge of the state's experience of the War is unlikely to be attainable: the purpose of this book is to attempt the beginning of such an history, with the hope that it will form a foothold for further interest in the study of the subject.

NOTES TO THE INTRODUCTION.

1. McAfee, Ward M. "California History Textbooks and the Coming of the Civil War: the Need for a Broader Perspective of California History," *Southern California Quarterly*. Vol. LVI., N° 2. Summer, 1974. pp. 159-175.
The texts examined in McAfee's essay are:.
Bean, Walton. California, *An Interpretive History*. New York. 1973.
Beck, Warren A., and David Williams. *California, an History of the Golden State*. New York. 1972.
Caughey, John W. *California, a Remarkable State's Life History*. 3d. ed. Englewood Cliffs, N. J. 1970.
Cleland, Robert Glass. *From Wilderness to Empire, an History of California*. Ed. Glenn S. Dumke. New York.1959.
Rolle, Andrew F. *California, an History*. New York. 1963.
Roske, Ralph. Euerymlin's Eden, *An History of California*. NewYork.1968.
2. Bancroft, Hubert Howe. *The Works of Hubert Howe Bancroft*,Vol. VII. *of History of California, 1860-1890*. The History Company Publishers. San Francisco. 1890.
3. Books examined include:-
Colton, Ray C. *The Civil War in the Western Territories*. Norman. 1959.
Hall, Martin Hardwick. *Sibley's New Mexico Campaign*. Boston. 1960.
Josephy, Alvin M., Jr. *The Civil War in the American West*. New York. 1991.
Kerby, Robert Lee. *The Confederate Invasion of New Mexico and Arizona, 1861-1862*. Los Angeles. 1958.
Lewis, Oscar. *The War in the Far West, 1861-1865*. Garden City. 1961.
4. Kennedy, Elijah R. *The Contest For California in 1861*. Houghton Mifflin Co. Boston. 1912. pp. 194-197.
5. Gilbert, Benjamin Franklin. "California and the Civil War: A Bibliographical Essay." *California Historical Society Quarterly*. Vol. XL. N°.4. 1961. pp. 289-290.

**CALIFORNIA
IN THE
WAR FOR SOUTHERN INDEPENDENCE.**

The State Split Line of 1860.

CALIFORNIA IN 1860, A MICROCOSM OF THE UNITED STATES.

An understanding of the nature and politics of the people of California is necessary for a just comprehension of the conflict within California during the War for Southern Independence; for such comprehension, it is necessary to understand, not the Native Americans or the Californios, but the North Americans who became Californians. It is also necessary to consider the vastly different geography, climate, and economies which existed within the state.

The population consisted of three significant groups: the Indians, who were being exterminated; the Californios, these being the Spanish settlers and their descendants who had come under Mexican jurisdiction until they and their lands were acquired by the United States at the end of the Mexican War in 1848; and the North Americans, who had immigrated to California over the years from the eastern states. The number of North Americans increased greatly after the discovery of gold in 1847.

Interest in California on the part of the United States began when the occupation of the territory became the ultimate goal of manifest destiny. The people of the United States believed it to be their God-given destiny to occupy the North American continent from sea to sea. President Andrew Jackson had made an offer to Mexico in 1837 to buy California from the 38th Parallel to Oregon Territory in order to obtain San Francisco Bay, but was unaware that San Francisco Bay lay some 12 miles south of that parallel.[1] The first Americans to appear in California were merchants from New England.

By 1808, the annexation of California by the United States was advocated by several leading politicians; in 1826, fur trappers from the southern frontier areas of Kentucky, Missouri, and Tennessee arrived. The first American settlers who put down roots were the New Englanders who began migrating to California by sea about 1818; they did not keep their identity as Americans, but became prosperous Mexican citizens, and often married into prominent Californio families.

By 1845, there was substantial immigration by covered waggon. The early pioneers encouraged others to follow; among them was Lansford W. Hastings, a frontier lawyer, who, in 1843, led a group of mercenaries into the Sacramento Valley with the idea of leading a revolt, like the recent Texan one, for the purpose of establishing a Pacific Republic, a new American state. To increase the North American population in California, Hastings published an error-filled tract, entitled, *Emigrants' Guide*. The inaccuracies of that publication caused serious difficulties for some pioneers. The flow of pioneers from the various states increased after 1848, when California became a part of the Mexican Cession to the United States.

The Congress of the United States provided no legal form of government from the end of the Mexican War in 1848 to the granting of statehood on September 9, 1850.[2] When General Bennett Riley, who had become "civil" governor in 1848, heard that Congress had adjourned in 1849 without agreement on territorial organization for California, he felt a stimulus was required, and, on June 3, 1849, issued a call for a Constitutional Convention to convene at Monterey on September 1 of that year. He knew this action was consistent with the attitude of President Zachary Taylor, who, as a Southern Unionist, felt California might break the deadlock over the territorial expansion of slavery if she were to confront the rest of the nation with a state organization and a constitution.[3]

The Constitutional Convention assembled on the appointed date to determine the direction the state would take. Of the 48 delegates who attended, 37 were from California's northern districts; most delegates had been in California for more than three years. The Convention sought to define California in legal terms; issues for decision included the determination of the borders of California, whether California would apply for admission as a state or a territory, and, if a state, whether slave or free, and the determination of those to whom suffrage would be granted.

The most difficult decision made by the delegates seemed to be that of the eastern boundary; the other three boundaries had already been established by Oregon, Mexico, and the Pacific Ocean. Some delegates sought to place the eastern boundary deep in the Mexican Cession, east of the Great Salt Lake; a majority of the delegates, however, were agreed that the U. S. Congress might reject the Californian Constitution if her boundaries were made too large, and feared a possible negative reaction at Washington to her petition for statehood; in the end, the present state boundaries were settled upon.[4]

A one-sided vote decided California would apply for admission as a state rather than a territory. The southern Californians favoured territorial status, because theirs was a land of ranchos; the prominent people owned land which could be taxed by a state, but the Federal Government provided funds in support of her territories. Northern California, with a population of about 120,000, was primarily engaged in mining and the industry essential to mining, neither of which meant taxable land ownership; thus, the South's population of about 6,000 would, in essence, provide funds for the entire state budget. The north favoured statehood, and the motion for statehood, made by Southerner William Gwin, was passed, even though every delegate from Southern California who was present voted against it.

A proposal was made by the southern Californians for a compromise, by which that part of California north of San Luis Obispo would become a state, and the southern part would become a territory. The majority from the north rejected the idea.[5] The notion of two separate states did not die, however, for, nine years later, in 1858, a bill that would have separated San Luis Obispo, Santa Barbara, San Bernardino, Los Angeles, and San Diego counties from the rest of the state, to form the Territory of Colorado, was introduced; the bill passed both houses of the Legislature, and, as a proposal on the ballot, was strongly ratified by the electorate of Southern California.[6] The vote of Californians south of Fresno was: for secession, 2,459; against, 828. Only San Luis Obispo County chose to stay with the north, 283 to 10.[7]

The division was supported by the governor of California, Milton S. Latham, who wrote President James Buchanan, "The Union of Southern and Northern California was unnatural." This union gave great dissatisfaction to the people of southern California, he wrote, because of "the inequality of taxation by reason of the failure of mining interests of the north to pay their fair proportion of taxes."

Years later, the opinion was expressed, by Robert S. Bulla in a paper of 1907, that the issue of slavery was the main motivation for the support of the proposed division.[8] This seems unlikely in view of the fact slavery was unanimously rejected at the Constitutional Convention of 1849, when California's distaste for slavery was made plain.

When the bill reached Washington, Congress had more pressing concerns over the possible extension of slavery and secession of the Southern states; the North in 1860 feared that, if either a new state or territory were to be created in California that favoured slavery, the slave-holding states would be strengthened by the acquisition of both new territory and an outlet to the Pacific Ocean.[9]

The Constitutional Convention of 1849 consisted of 20 delegates from the northern part of the state, 17 from the southern part of the state, eight native Californians, and three of foreign birth [10] who represented Californians from various parts of the United States. The rejection of slavery by the people of California was strongly expressed by the delegates; the delegate from Coloma, William E. Shannon, made the motion to prohibit slavery. To the surprise of many, the delegates unanimously voted for California to apply for admission to the Union as a free state; that vote, of course, included the yeas of all 17 of the delegates who had come from states which, not twelve years later, were to enter the Confederacy. Among them was William Gwin, an avid spokesman for the South, who suggested California's constitution be based on that of the free state of Iowa, "because it was one of the latest and shortest."[11] A possible reason for the lack of opposition from delegates of Southern origin to the status of free state was the fact that less than one third of the citizens of the Southern states owned slaves, and were mostly small farmers who had no stake in what Southern leaders referred to as their "Peculiar Institution."[12] While southern California may well have chosen to join the Confederacy at a later time by virtue of having a culture more compatible with the Southern states than with that of northern California, slavery was never a cultural bond.

The overwhelming sentiment for the exclusion of slavery from California did not derive from humanitarian considerations; the Convention was not a gathering of abolitionists. Just before the Convention, a group of Texans had come to the Yuba River with a number of black slaves who had been brought to work the mining claims of their masters. Californian miners, whether from the north or the south, were outraged at the idea that gold mining was appropriate work for black slaves; the Texans were given notice that the slaves were to be clear of the district within hours. The delegate to the Constitutional Convention who represented the Yuba River District introduced the Constitutional provision that "neither slavery nor involuntary servitude, unless for the punishment of crimes, shall ever be tolerated in this state."

There was a proposal to exclude free blacks, as well as slaves, from California. It was asserted by a Sacramento delegate, of Kentuckian origin, that many owners of slaves were planning to bring them to California and free them on the condition they work the mines as indentured servants; he further asserted that free blacks were "idle in their habits, difficult to be governed by laws, thriftless, and uneducated," and that their presence in California would be an evil "greater than slavery itself." The exclusion clause was actually adopted, and would have remained in the Constitution, but for the primary concern, mentioned earlier with regard to the eastern boundary, that the inclusion of anything which might delay the full establishment of "a proper form of state government and its national recognition" should be avoided.[13]

Even among those of Southern birth who had no fear of blacks working in the state, there was a reluctance to permit their introduction. A letter written on June 28, 1851, by Judge Benjamin Hayes, who was living in Los Angeles, to his wife who was coming to join him, discouraged her from bringing a black child. His letter also makes plain the lack of a black population in Los Angeles:

> Tell Grace her child would be quite a curiosity here, a young lion (or lioness, I forget which). If you should not bring her, do not sell her; give her to one of your sisters, as they live in a slave state, or set her free, as you judge proper.[14]

In 1859, the power to deny suffrage on the grounds of race was still within constitutional authority. Indians were disenfranchised, even those Californios of mixed Indian and European blood; most Mexican Californians had some Indian ancestry, and had, along with full-blooded Indians, enjoyed suffrage under Mexican law, but the Californian Constitution extended the right to vote only to white, male citizens:[15] the decisions of statehood would be made by them.

California was granted statehood on September 9, 1850, as a free state, which act upset the balance of power in the Senate between the free and the slave states. The admission of California was the cause of the Compromise of 1850, which destroyed the Missouri Compromise, produced the Fugitive Slave Law, and generally increased tensions between the North and the South.

In 1852, a state census counted 223,856 Californians of non-Indian blood. The 1860 national census counted 380,000 such persons. There was but a small number of women in that group; California's birth rate was thus smaller than her death rate. The increase in population was the result of the arrival of immigrants,[16] mostly from other parts of the United States, who brought their local notions and social biases with them. This milieu of national political and philosophical notions guided the course of the state, and so California became a microcosm of the United States in political and cultural diversity.[17]

There was the industrial North and the agricultural South, with their divergent interests. Migrants came from both sections, and tended to settle in the part of California that most closely resembled home: Southerners settled in southern California to farm or practice professions in Los Angeles or small towns; some rose to important positions of leadership. Northerners tended to settle in the mining and industrial regions in and around San Francisco, where many of them became powerful leaders. More immigrants came from the populous northern states than the spacious .south; an exception to that pattern was the mass migration to the gold fields during the years of the Gold Rush. That quest for wealth included all regions and classes, from unwashed ruffians to gentlemen adventurers of worldwide origins. A popular song of the period in California was *What Was Your Name in the States?* The inference was that many of the immigrants were fugitives from the law; there is, however, another message in the song in its unspoken acknowledgment that those in California were not in the United States, that immigrants of any stripe were expatriates.[18]

It may be asked if the political bias that immigrants brought with them was solely North-South, slave economy or free-labour economy. As discussed above, there existed little racial liberalism on the part of Californians; slavery was, however, a point of disagreement that was not sharply divided along Northern and Southern lines. Northern industrialists were profiting greatly from slave-produced cotton in their New England mills, and, although many northerners, especially from the Midwest, opposed the extension of slavery into the territories, they did not care to interfere with it where it already existed. Most Californians found themselves in that category. All of the territory bordering California on the east, namely, Utah and New Mexico, was opened to slavery by the Compromise of 1850. Slavery was hardly an issue that would set Californians against one another in a war, or, for that matter, against the Union.

What, then, did define California's differences? They were set by the longtime national conflicts, exclusive of slavery, that were carried to California by the immigrants from the North and the South.

One of the most important differences in political thought was the concept of states' rights. The United States began under the Articles of Confederation; that document provided for a loose confederation of states with a central government with no power over commerce or the levying of taxes, and no federal courts. Any amendment required unanimity of the sovereign states.[19] After ratification of the United States Constitution by the last state in 1790, a federal government was established. Jeffersonian Democrats, nonetheless, continued to believe that, even under a federal constitution, a weak central government was desirable in order to preserve the rights of the states. Those of that political belief held also to a strict interpretation of the Constitution, meaning that all powers not specifically granted to the Federal government belonged to the states. The Republican Party, on the other hand, as did the Federalists and Whigs before them, believed in a powerful central government at the expense of the rights of the states, holding what the Constitution did not forbid, it permitted. This view gave the central government formidable powers.[20]

Another main difference in American thinking arose over a protective tariff that gave Northern industry a market without competition within the United States; the tariff gave northern industry high profits at the expense of southern and western agriculture. The latter were forced to pay higher prices for manufactured goods than such as would be charged if foreign competition had been permitted to exist.

Californians felt independent from faraway Washington, and had absolutely nothing to gain from the high protective tariff which was one of the foundations of the Republican Party; as a result, California was, politically speaking, a Democratic state.

The financial structure controlled by the northeast was considered an enemy by southern and western farmers, who paid high interest on loans they were forced to make for the harvest of their crops, and often lost their farms through foreclosure when crops failed. The Democratic Party had traditionally favoured cheap money to help debtors; the Republican Party supported the gold standard.

Another dispute between North and South was that of the route to be taken by the transcontinental railway; the failure before 1860 to build that railway had thus been a result of the sectional struggle. Northerners insisted the road be laid on free soil; Southerners had supported a route from the Southern states across Texas to a point touching the Pacific in southern California. With natural advantages of a shorter route, grading, and climate, this was the most practical proposed route across the continent. The Gadsden Purchase, bought from Mexico for ten million dollars in 1853, had been made specifically to obtain land for the southern route; it added a piece of land about the size of South Carolina to New Mexico Territory, and extended from the Colorado River to El Paso.[21]

In all of these issues, the South and the West had been championed by a Democratic Party which had been a unified national party until 1860. Democrats carried California in the election of 1856, even though California's popular John C. Fremont was the first Republican presidential candidate that year; in 1860, the Republicans nominated Abraham Lincoln against a deeply divided Democratic Party. The Democratic Northern wing was led by Stephen Douglass, who had been rejected by the Southern wing as a traitor to party principles; the Southern wing nominated Vice President John Breckinridge. Another Democratic faction formed the Constitutional Union Party out of concern for the preservation of the Union; they nominated John Bell. A national Democratic Party had ceased to exist.

In California, the significant Democratic contenders were the Douglass Democrats and the Chivalry, or "Chiv" Democrats, who supported the South. Lincoln carried the national election with 39.79 percent of the popular vote; he won only 10 of California's 44 counties, most of them in the more densely-populated areas around San Francisco. Breckinridge carried 17 counties, Douglass the remaining seven. San Francisco cast a total of 14,350 votes, Los Angeles 1,737. Even with such an imbalance between the centres of power of the northern and southern parts of the state, Lincoln won with 32 percent of the popular vote. Breckinridge carried both Los Angeles and San Diego Counties.[22] Lincoln won California, but not two-thirds of her voters.

Lincoln was the first sectional president; his support in California came from a minority who were former Whigs, Free Soilers, and Abolitionists, that is, the components which had created the Republican Party of the North. A Union led by their political fellows indeed represented a victory that would allow legislation to be passed that they had long sought. Some California Democrats, especially amongst the Douglass faction, felt obliged to maintain the Union even under a hostile administration. As expressed by the editor of the *The Herald*, a Breckinridge-supporting Ukiah newspaper, secession, this meaning revolution, is justified when an unbearable government holds power that permits no recourse for change. Whilst acknowledging the Republican administration would attempt to carry out the extreme doctrines of those whom the editor called the ultra-abolitionists of the North, he did not believe Lincoln would do so, because Lincoln had pledged he would not implement those doctrines, and stated he had no sympathy for ultra-abolitionists; even if the Republicans were successful, however, there was a better way to remedy the evil: the use of the elective franchise. Secession by dissatisfied states would lead to civil wars and bloody strife between men of kindred origin, and, finally, perhaps the annihilation of the weaker party; it would destroy a useful government. By using the ballot box, corrections might be made in the next year or two.[23]

Many Californians from Southern states involved in secession, the border states, and others of similar beliefs, felt no allegiance to Lincoln's administration or the section that it represented. The ratification of the Constitution, which had been given voluntarily, was rescinded by each seceding state before the act of secession; some Californians of southern origin felt obliged to defend their home states from Lincoln's invading armies.

The Californios themselves felt little affection for, or allegiance to, the Union; many Californians felt abandoned by Washington, as did the people of Arizona Territory before her secession. The idea of a Pacific Republic had been debated, without rancour; before the election of 1860; after the Republican ascension, some Californians identified with that idea, and considered the possibility of aligning such a republic with the Confederacy.[24]

Those Californians who were adamantly opposed to a sectional administration feared that it would create lasting institutions; they recalled the Declaration of Independence, written when people sought separation from a government that they felt was foreign and oppressive —

When, in the course of human events, it becomes necessary for one people to dissolve the political bonds which have connected them with another. …

Governments are instituted among men, deriving their just powers from the consent of the governed; that whenever any form of government becomes destructive of these ends, it is the right of the people to alter or to abolish it, and to institute new government.

The South felt overwhelmed and abused by Northern power, which would most certainly increase under a Northern administration, and thus thought —

But, when a long train of abuses and usurpations, pursuing invariably the same object, evinces a design to reduce them under absolute despotism, it is their right, it is their duty, to throw off such government.[25]

In summary, California's population were divided, like the rest of the nation, from the election of 1860 to the outbreak of the War; the reasons for the division, with the exception of slavery, were the same as those that divided the nation as a whole. The exploits of Californians who supported the Union have been well recorded by historians; those who supported the Confederacy have been given only fleeting, and often hostile, recognition: but who were they, and how did their convictions guide their actions?

NOTES TO CHAPTER I.

1. James J. Rawls and Walton Bean. *California: An Interpretive History*. McGraw-Hill. San Francisco. 1988. p. 69.
2. Rawls and Bean, p. 96.
3. Rawls and Bean, p. 97:
4. Rawls and Bean, p. 99.
5. Rawls and Bean, p. 98.
6. Rosaline Levinson. "State Splitting Saga Rolls On." *California Historian*. Vol. 40. N°1. September, 1993. p. 9.
7. *Native Son*. September/October, 1993. Vol. 2. Cols. 1-2.

8. Levinson, p. 10.
9. Levinson, p. 10.
10. J. N. Bowman. "The Original Constitution of California of 1849." *California Historical Society Quarterly*. Vol. 28. N°2. June, 1949. pp. 193-197.
11. Donovan Lewis. "Admission Day and Statehood." *The Native Son*. August-September, 1987. p. 4.
12. Kevin H. Siepel. *Rebel*. St. Martin's Press. New York. 1983. p. 7.
13. Rawls and Bean, pp. 98-99.
14. Benjamin Ignatius Hayes. *Pioneer Notes*. Ed. Marjorie Tisdale Wolcott. McBride Printing Company. Los Angeles. 1929. p. 75.
15. Rawls and Bean, pp. 98-99.
16. Rawls and Bean, p. 146.
17. Melvin Panizza. "Political System Failure: California, 1860." 1971 MS. Holt-Atherton Library Special Collection, University of the Pacific, Stockton, California. November 29, 1971. pp. 2-3.
18. Bailey, Thomas P., and David M. Kennedy. *The American Pageant*. D.C. Heath and Company. Lexington. 1994. p. 408.
19. Bailey and Kennedy, p. 175.
20. Bailey and Kennedy, pp. 187-189.
21. W. H. Watford. "Confederate Western Ambitions." *The Southwestern Historical Quarterly*. Vol. 44. N° 2. June, 1944. pp. 193-197.
22. *The Herald*. Ukiah, Cal. December 14, 1860. Vol. II. Col. 3.
23. *The Herald*. Vol. II. Col.1.
24. Conmy, Peter T. "The Pacific Republic." *The Grizzly Bear*. Vol. 66. January, 1940. p. 3.
25. The Declaration of Independence in Congress, July 4, 1776. First paragraph.

CHAPTER II. ALBERT SIDNEY JOHNSTON.

Albert Sidney Johnston was one of many who left California to serve the Confederate States of America. Born a Southerner in Kentucky, Johnston entered the United States Army, transferring to the new Republic of Texas in 1836 as the revolutionary army's senior brigadier general in the war with Mexico for the Republic's independence. After the revolution, he served as Secretary of War for the Republic of Texas from 1838 to 1840; later, he became a gentleman planter. He is, therefore, considered by many to be a Texan rather than a Californian.

However, a strong case may be made, for two reasons, to consider Albert Sidney Johnston a Californian: first, before his decision to go south after suffering Federal harassment, he intended to become a civilian resident of California, and make a living there; secondly, his wife's family, the Griffins, were prominent residents of Los Angeles. It is certainly probable that, had the general survived the war, he would have rejoined his family near Los Angeles. The general, born in Kentucky, had two adopted states, Texas and California. California was his last state of residence, and remained that of his family.

Californians of Southern heritage or sympathy responded in various ways to President Lincoln's call of April 15, 1861, to state governors, for 75,000 men join with the regular army to suppress the secession of seven Southern states.[1]

In February, 1861, eight of the fifteen Southern states remained in the Union. On February 8, representatives of the seven seceding states met at Montgomery, Alabama, adopted a constitution, and elected Jefferson Davis as president of the Confederate States of America.[2] Abraham Lincoln was inaugurated as president of the United States on March 4, 1861, but, even before Lincoln took office, the issues of his presidential campaign became obsolete. The great question was no longer whether territories would be slave or free, but the acceptability of the withdrawal of states from the Union. Lincoln, an ardent nationalist, believed the Union should stand as she was; if the Union were to be maintained, however, an aggressive war would have to be waged, which was favoured by few northerners. The Confederacy had much to lose, and nothing to gain, by war; it was in the best interest of the Confederacy merely to preserve herself as an independent state, a status that existed in peace, but could be lost in war.[3]

Lincoln's decision to send a fleet for the relief of Fort Sumter gave him the end that he sought; the Confederates fired on Sumter on the morning of April 12, and thus convicted themselves by an act of aggression.

Albert Sidney Johnston.

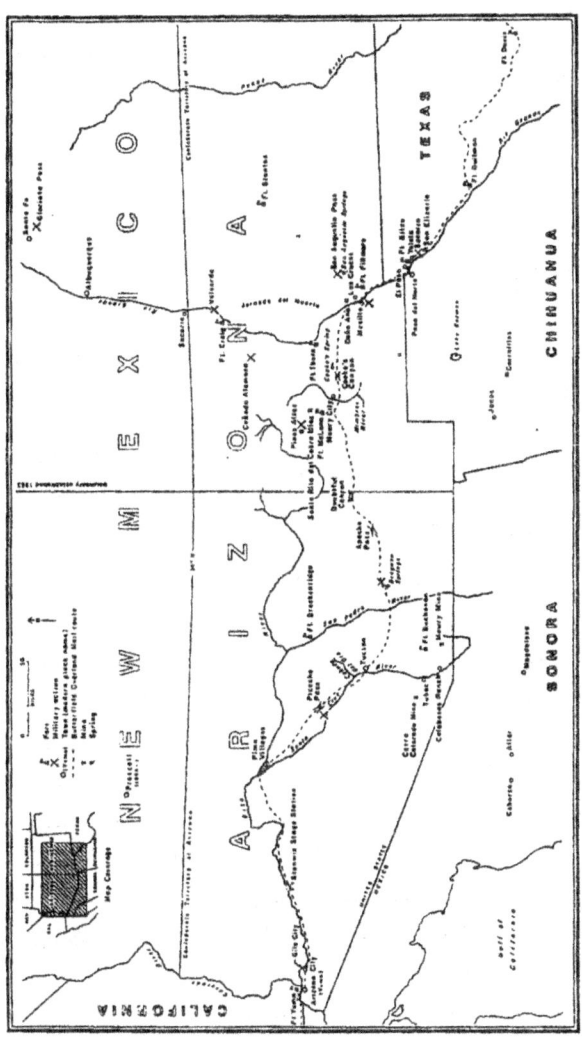

Map of the Itinerary Taken by The Johnston Party
from California to Texas.

As Lincoln's friend, Orville Browning, a senator from Illinois, wrote in his diary: "The plan succeeded; they attacked Sumter — it fell, and thus did more service than it otherwise could." Before the attack on Sumter, there was no more unanimity in the North on waging war than there had been in the South on secession. After the attack on Sumter, Lincoln might wage war and speak of it as a defensive war; he had given the South no option, for the fort had to be attacked by the Confederacy, or abandoned by the Union forces, to maintain the logic of secession.[4]

When the conflict began, doubts vanished, and there was a great amount of war fever in both the North and the South. Lincoln called for volunteers, whereupon Virginia, North Carolina, Arkansas, and Tennessee seceded, and rebellion broke out in Maryland. The balance of power was held by the remaining border states. Maryland and Delaware were held in the Union by their proximity to Northern military power and their immediate military occupation by Federal forces. Keeping Missouri and Kentucky out of the Confederacy was more difficult.[5] Unionists there were not separated into two clearly defined areas, for the loyalties of the populations of large border areas were torn. The populations of Maryland, Kentucky, Missouri, Delaware, and the western portions of Virginia were divided in their sentiments toward the Union and the Confederacy. Even the southern parts of Ohio, Indiana, and Illinois favoured the South in some measure; many of the regions were uncertain which way to turn.[6]

The situation was the same in the microcosm of the nation that was California. Like the border states, California supplied troops to both the Union and the Confederacy.[7] Many Californians believed there would be no war to coerce the South back into the Union. Although many of Southern sympathy opposed secession, most felt the Southern states had the right to secede. Lincoln's declaration of war to destroy a new nation many Americans believed to be lawful and legitimate[8] caused many Californians to search their conscience in forming a decision as to whom to give their loyalty.

Several prominent Californians left the state to fight for the South as a matter of conscience; probably the best known was Albert Sidney Johnston. Johnston was born at the village of Washington in Mason County, Kentucky, and was an 1826 graduate of West Point. He fought in the Black Hawk War of 1832, but, two years later, resigned from the army. He joined the Texan Army in their revolt against Mexico, and became Adjutant General, and afterwards Secretary of War, of the Republic of Texas; he left this position to join Zachary Taylor and fight in the Mexican War. When the war ended, Johnston resigned from the army to manage his plantation in

Brazoria County, Texas; his tenure as a planter was, however, short lived, and, in 1851, he was back in the army.[9] He would later become a resident of Los Angeles, and could have had a ranch on the site of what is now the City of Pasadena, had he chosen to do so.[10] His wife was the sister of Dr. John S. Griffin, an eminent physician and surgeon of Los Angeles, who was a native of Virginia.[11] Griffin had served as Health Officer for the City of Los Angeles, and was paid with 2,000 acres of what became East Los Angeles.[12]

In 1860, when the sectional controversy became intense, Johnston refused the offer of command of the Department of the Southwest because he was concerned that Texas, one of his home states, would secede; nonetheless, he did not want to be disloyal to a government that had confidence in him. General Winfield Scott supported his assignment to command the Department of the Pacific.[13] Brevet Brigadier General Albert Sidney Johnston complied with General Order No. 10, of November 22, 1860, which put him in command of the Department of the Pacific. The department was formed at that time by merging the Departments of California and Oregon.

Johnston seemed to have made a clean break with Texas; his family would accompany him to California, and he granted his son, William Preston, power of attorney to sell all of his Texas lands. He owned two slaves, and, as California was a free state, he left one with his son, and the other, Ran (Randolph Hughes), who wished to accompany the Johnston family to California, was emancipated.

The Johnstons were most impressed with California; he praised San Francisco's schools and climate. Mrs. Johnston desired her children to make their lives in California, saying that California was a thriving country, free of internal strife.[14] The general arrived at his San Francisco headquarters on January 15, 1861.[15]

He was torn inwardly; for years, he had feared for the Union because of sectional controversy. South Carolina had seceded from the Union while the Johnstons were on the journey to California, and the six lower Southern states, including Texas, followed South Carolina's lead. Johnston was an ardent nationalist who felt sorrow because of the South's action, even though he firmly believed any sovereign state had the right to withdraw from a union she had voluntarily entered. He hoped still the Union might be peacefully preserved, and echoed the sentiments of the great Union meeting that was held at San Francisco, saying, "I would that there were no other sentiments within the broad expanse of our country."[16] He made it clear to his friends and family that, whilst honour demanded that he remain faithful to the United States as long as he held his commission in the United States Army, his heart was with the South. He decided he could not command United States troops in an invasion of Texas; if, therefore, Texas entered the Confederacy, he would feel obliged to resign his commission.[17]

During his command of the Department of the Pacific, General Johnston served well, and obeyed his orders from Washington, which included his participation in military negotiations with the British in Canada.[18] He strengthened the defences of the harbour of San Francisco, and stored weapons at Fort Alcatraz for security; he increased efforts at recruitment so as to keep the forces of the Department of the Pacific at full strength.[19] On March 23, 1861, Johnston directed military operations against "predatory Indians" in Humboldt County and Washington Territory from his headquarters at San Francisco.[20]

Unknown to Johnston as he attended to the duties of his command, nervous Unionists in San Francisco who were aware of his Southern sympathy had communicated their fears to powerful people in Washington; they feared Johnston would turn traitor at the first opportunity.[21] Various rumours were spread that Johnston was part of a plot hatched around the San Francisco Bay to conquer California and force the state to secede. Johnston was rumoured to have been placed in command to initiate a series of moves that would take over military installations, convert the military forces in California into a secessionist army, and form a Pacific Republic.[22]

So prevalent became the rumours of Johnston's involvement in a Southern conspiracy in California, that Governor John G. Downey expressed his qualms to the general. Johnston assured the governor the fortifications and arms of the Pacific Department were safe; he ended his letter of assurance to Governor Downey with these words: "I have been long identified with Texas, her interests and public men, and her action may control my destiny. But, in any event, I shall give due notice and turn over intact my department to my successor."

On April 9, 1861, Johnston received information that a Texas convention had carried into effect their own earlier decision, supported by a popular referendum, to withdraw from the Union and join the Confederacy. Until that time, Johnston had believed the Southern States, through joint action, might obtain from the North sufficient guaranties to make secession unnecessary, and the Union could be preserved: he knew now; however; that "the persistent obstinacy of the Republican party, in refusing to concede anything whatever for the sake of the Union," indicated that the South "seems instinctively to have seized the right conclusion."[23]

The rumours of his disloyalty had reached Lincoln, and, on March 23, 1861, the president's secretary ordered, Brigadier General Edwin V Sumner to California to replace Johnston. It was apparently done with some attempt at secrecy, because, before the official order dated March 23, 1861, a letter of March 22 cautioned that the order for Albert Sidney Johnston's replacement remain unpublished "for confidential reasons" until Sumner was at sea. In view of the circumstances, it is reasonable to assume that some in Washington feared that Johnston, having a knowledge of his coming relief from command, would turn over his department to Confederate activists; the War Department seemed, however, to have given him the benefit of the doubt, because Sumner's orders, which were to be presented to Johnston at San Francisco, commanded the General to return to Washington to receive further orders.[24] The letter to Johnston stated that he had the confidence of the Secretary of War, and would receive an important command upon his arrival.[25]

In spite of the concern of the Unionists, Johnston, described by a San Franciscan as "a blond giant of a man with a mass of heavy yellow hair untouched by age, although he was nearing 60," carried out his duties loyally. Although he thought the fear of a secessionist coup was exaggerated, he secured his command, to guard it against surprise. Before Sumner reached San Francisco, Johnston, on April 8, 1861, learned Texas had joined the Confederacy. The next day, he sent his letter of resignation to Washington. Scrupulously faithful to his trust whilst he held his commission, he wrote to his son, "My escutcheon is without a blur upon it, and never will be tarnished."[26]

On April 25, 1861, Sumner presented his papers to Johnston, and assumed command of the department.[27] He stated in a letter to Army Headquarters that the command was turned over to him in good order, and, although Johnston had forwarded his resignation earlier, Johnston continued to hold the command, and was carrying out the orders of the government.[28] In the following days, Johnston learned for the first time the administration had doubted his loyalty; he was outraged to learn he had not been trusted, and expressed satisfaction over having already resigned. On May 6, 1861, the War Department formally approved his resignation.

When Johnston left the service, he seems to have intended to remain neutral and not give service to either side; he wrote that he would accept any form of civilian employment that would support his family. After he was relieved of command, he joined the Griffins at Los Angeles, intending to remain passive in California, intending to buy a rancho near that of his brother-in-law, Dr. Griffin; he grew restless, however, after the firing on Fort Sumter had made war inevitable, and the raising of armies in both the North and the South.

After a month of conflicting emotions and soul searching, Johnston resolved to join the army of the Confederacy.[29] At once strongly Southern and strongly unionist, he regarded with aversion the Republican Party, which was anti-Southern, and, in inception and tendency, dis-unionist; he believed the sovereignty of the states was the backbone of national liberties, and was to be carefully respected and defended. He had learned from the Declaration of Independence "the inherent right of every people to select their own form of government, and to maintain their independence by revolution."

Secession was not war, and Texas ardently desired peace. If peace were maintained, his son Preston wrote, "He would retire to some small farm near Los Angeles, California, and, among congenial friends, far from the strife of faction, would pass the evening of his days in tranquility … and in the balmy air of that garden of the West, he would nurture his children in scenes unvisited by civil discord."

General Johnston remained at Los Angeles from May 2, 1861, until his departure on June 16; whilst contemplating a peaceful life in California, aloof from the sectional conflict, Johnston's life became, as his son wrote, "one of anxiety, difficulty, and danger. … Soldiers had been sent to Los Angeles to watch his movements," and "he was virtually a prisoner in the department that he had lately commanded." He came to the conclusion that the same reasons for which he had resigned his commission, namely, his love of Texas and the South, were strong enough to cause him to return to Southern soil and act on his beliefs. His original plan to sail with his family to New York was abandoned because friends had warned him he was to be arrested if he tried to leave California.[30]

The War Department was not aware of any of Johnston's plans to leave California, or of a route that he might take. On June 3, 1861, General Winfield Scott wrote to Colonel H. L. Scott at New York, instructing him to arrest Johnston if he arrived in New York Harbour; the army did not apparently want the arrest of Johnston made public, and so it was suggested to Colonel Scott that Johnston be arrested aboard ship and brought ashore by means of a pilot boat. In another letter, also dated June 3, 1861, Winfield Scott instructed the commanding officer of the Department of the West at St. Louis, Missouri, to arrest Johnston if he left California by an overland route.[31]

Alonzo Ridley was Undersheriff of Los Angeles County and captain of the Los Angeles Mounted Rifles, a brigade of the California Militia; from their inception, the Los Angeles Mounted Rifles were pro-Southern. Ridley, although of northern birth, was deeply impressed with the righteousness of the Southern cause;[32] after the war, the organizers of the Rifles, Ridley and George Gift, acknowledged the purpose of the unit had been to serve the Confederacy. The unit of militia had been well armed by the State of California, owing largely to Governor Downey's response to Captain Ridley's request for pistols, rifles, and sabres, which included the arms from other units of militia then defunct.[33]

With the outbreak of the War, news of which did not reach Los Angeles until April 24, any service of the Rifles to the Confederacy seemed unlikely, and so the means by which the unit might become a part of the Confederate Army were considered; Ridley decided that the best plan would be to march across the desert to Texas, following the same route previously taken by individuals and small parties.[34]

Captain Ridley, well aware of General Johnston's intent to offer his services to the Confederacy, encountered Dr. Griffin, the general's brother-in-law, on a street in Los Angeles, and offered him the services of the Los Angeles Mounted Rifles to help the general reach the Confederacy. Johnston and Ridley met at Dr. Griffin's office on the following day, and the general accepted Ridley's offer.[35] Since Johnston was under constant watch, the necessary preparations for his departure fell to Randolph Hughes, the former slave who functioned as Johnston's servant and bodyguard.[36]

Ridley had planned to leave on June 30, but, having learned both he and Johnston were facing imminent arrest on charges of treason, he, Johnston, and Hughes left Los Angeles early on the morning of June 16 for Chino Ranch, about thirty miles east of Los Angeles. The proprietor of the ranch, Robert S. Carlisle, was a private in the Los Angeles Mounted Rifles. Ridley left Johnston in order to inform the rest of his party the departure was under way, and that the main body were to assemble at Warner's Ranch in San Diego County. Warner's Ranch was owned by another private of the Los Angeles Mounted Rifles, John Rains. At Chino, Private Carman Frazee joined the General and Hughes, and guided them to Warner's Ranch. Carlisle posted his vaqueros along the route to watch for Union troops and warn the party in case they should be detected.[37]

Most of the group which would march to Texas had assembled at Warner's Ranch by June 26. Johnston was offered command, but declined, saying that he was no longer a general, but a citizen who would serve under Ridley. The party included six lieutenants who had resigned from the

Muster Roll of the Los Angeles Mounted Rifles

Organized March 7th 1861, in the County of Los Angeles and State of California in accordance with the Militia Laws of said State.

Division _____ Brigade _____
California Militia

Officers

Commissioned:

Alonzo Ridley	Captain
Joseph W. Callick	1st Lieut.
Tomas A. Sanchez	2d Lieut.
Samuel Ayres	2d Lieut.

Non Commissioned:—

Sergeants
- Robert A. Hester
- Pedro Antº Abila
- Francis M. Chapman
- Joseph N. Chandler

Corporals
- Joseph Huber Jr.
- Rafael S. Bauchet
- Lyman A. Smith
- Francisco Martinez

First Page of the Muster Roll
of The Los Angeles Mounted Rifles in Early 1861.

Privates

1. Abila, Jose Maria
2. Alexander, F.H.
3. Abbott, Wm
4. Allen, Gabe
5. Allen, O.C.
6. Ayers, C.R.
7. Brust, J.S.
8. Brundige, M.D.
9. Bunchel, Pew. G.
10. Beldemain, Joseph
11. Bowers, Wm
12. Beale, Walter S.
13. Carlos, James W.
14. Carey, Wm P.
15. Cota, Manl.
16. Cota, Francisco
17. Carlisle, Robt. S.
18. Duffy, Wm B.
19. Frazee, C.
20. Gift, Geo W.
21. Hardy, C.A.
22. Hardy, A.U.
23. Hollingsworth, M.G.
24. Hodges, Francis M.
25. Hidden, E. Wl
26. Jordan, L. Jr
27. Jackim, Lew

28. Lynn, Early
29. Mott, J.D.
30. McKenzie, Dove
31. Moore, Enoch
32. Myles, H.R.
33. McDaniels, Alf.
34. McKennan, W.
35. Newmark, M.J.
36. Murrll, J.G.
37. Northrup, James
38. Perez, Jose
39. Phelps, A.H.
40. Parker, James L.
41. Rains, John
42. Ruiz, Alonzo
43. Show, Wm H
44. Stelim, Wm W
45. Schaeffer, Henry
46. Stonehouse, Tom
47. Stark, Jesse
48. Stevens, B.H.
49. Spencer, A.J.
50. Sanchez, Felipe
51. Sanchez, Guadalupe
52. Sanchez, Jose ant°
53. Skinner, Wm. Wl.
54. Shaw, J.W.

Second Page of the Muster Roll
of The Los Angeles Mounted Rifles in Early 1861.

Laurence F. Talbott, PhD

55 Sylvar, Jesse
56 Swain, J. C.
57 Thomas, Chas. B.
58 Trafford, Thomas
59 Welsh, J. C.
60 Wickham, Thomas N.
61 Wygal, Warren
62 Workman, E. H.
63 Wiley, H. C.
64 Warren, Wm. C.

State of California,
County of Los Angeles.

I, Alonzo Ridley, Captain of the Volunteer Military Company, called the "Los Angeles Mounted Rifles," do hereby certify that the above and foregoing is a full, true and correct Muster Roll of said Company. Given under my hand at the City of Los Angeles this 9th of March A.D. 1861.

Alonzo Ridley
Captain

Third Page of the Muster Roll
of The Los Angeles Mounted Rifles in Early 1861.

U.S. Army, and taken the same position as Johnston, becoming, in effect, privates in the Rifles. In Vallecito, about thirty-five miles from Warner's Ranch, the party were joined by Major Lewis S. Armistead, also resigned from the U. S. Army, and his brother, Walker Keith Armistead. The party now consisted of Albert Sidney Johnston, Randolph Hughes, seven resigned army officers, twenty-six troopers of the Los Angeles Mounted Rifles, and the Major's brother, a total of thirty-six men.[39]

The party left Vallecito on June 30, crossed the Colorado River on July 4, and reached Tucson, which was under Confederate control, on July 18.[40] They were made welcome by the citizens of Tucson, where three more men enlisted in the Rifles. The Californians rode into Mesilla, the capital of Confederate Arizona Territory, on July 28, 1861, and were warmly welcomed by Colonel John Robert Baylor. Colonel Baylor, on August 1, proclaimed himself governor of the Confederate Territory of Arizona. It was at Mesilla that the march of the Los Angeles Mounted Rifles and those who accompanied them ended.[41]

The official records list only the names of the seven resigned officers that accompanied Johnston, along with thirty unnamed Confederate Army volunteers; this information was obtained from a letter written by F. W. Pickens of Columbia, South Carolina, to the President of the Confederate States, Jefferson Davis. He wrote that Johnston's party had crossed the Colorado River on July 1, 1861, but the correct date was July 4, 1861.[42] More detailed information was printed in the *Messilla Times* in August, 1861, in a front page article, entitled, "Arrival of Californians." The article provides the name, rank, and late military unit of each of the resigned officers, including Johnston, as well as the names of each of the volunteers,[43] and concludes with the following.

This company, excluding the ex-army officers, was organized in California for the purpose of repairing to the seat of the war in Virginia, there to take part in the-war now progressing. They will march in a few days for San Antonio, and from thence proceed with all possible dispatch to Memphis, Tennessee, and Richmond.

Baylor tendered to Johnston the command of his forces, which Johnston accepted.[44] Baylor's deferential offer was to give Johnston temporary command of his brigade, and Baylor wrote of his act on September 21, 1861:

Here I was joined by Brig. Gen. A. S. Johnston with a party of officers of the U.S. Army who had resigned and were en route for Richmond, Virginia; also a party of Californians under Capt. Alonzo Ridley. I tendered

The Johnston Party Crossing the Desert.

to Brigadier General Johnston the command of my forces, believing that the interest of the service required that I should relinquish the command to an officer of his rank and distinguished ability, which he did me the honour to accept, and remained in command until there was no further necessity for hi services.[45]

After that delay, Johnston, Ridley, the two Armisteads, and Hughes took a stage to El Paso. It was at Mesilla that the Los Angeles Mounted Rifles disbanded, but the members served the Confederacy in separate units on many battlefields.[46]

The Johnston party had crossed 800 miles through the hottest and driest regions of North America, where temperatures could reach 120 degrees; there was little shade on the rocky wasteland and drifting sand. Water was scarce, there was no relief.[47] This remarkable group is usually called simply "Johnston's Escort" by those writers who mention them at all; however, a Californian unit of militia that undertook such a journey under their commanding officer to join the Army of the Confederate States, and provide safe passage for a general soon to become highly distinguished in the Confederate service, participated in an historic event worthy of note.[48]

There are several sources that provide a muster of those who crossed the desert with Johnston; the names vary somewhat in spelling, and, in some cases, they are listed by only one source. The roster that is reproduced in this book is the best the author could find from available information.

Some of Johnston's party completed their journey to Richmond, where he was given the rank of general in the army of the Confederate States. After Johnston had left the state, Californian secessionists organized in many counties of southern California, and made preparations to receive a Confederate Army of Liberation.[49] There was concern among Unionists that Johnston would command the Confederate western forces and capture New Mexico as well as Arizona;[50] he was also rumoured to be planning to capture both Yuma, Arizona, and Sonora, Mexico. This rumour was referred to in a letter to the Secretary of State, William Seward, from Clarence E. Bennett of San Bernardino, California, who wrote about rebellion in that county.[51]

Johnston did not return west from Richmond, but was given command of Confederate forces at Shiloh in western Tennessee during the battle fought there on April 6-7, 1862.[52] He was killed in action on April 6, 1862, when a minie ball struck him in the calf of the leg. Disdaining care for the wound, Johnston remained in the saddle, commanding his men, until he died from loss of blood.[53] The death of Johnston was considered a great blow to the Confederacy by the South, as he had come to be recognised as a formidable military leader.[54] Captain Alonzo Ridley remained with Johnston until Johnston's death, and continued serving in the Texas Cavalry as a major of the 3rd Arizona Regiment; he was later promoted to a colonel.[55]

NOTES TO CHAPTER II.

1. Goldman, Henry H. "Southern Sympathy in Southern California 1860-1865." *Journal of the West*. Vol. IV. N° 4. October, 1965. p. 57 4.
2. Canby, Cortland, ed. *Lincoln and the. Civil War*. George Braziller, Inc. New York. 1960. p. 43.
3. Canby, pp. 56-57.
4. Canby, pp. 58-59.
5. Canby, pp. 60-64.
6. Canby, p. 48.
7. Hil, Laurence L. 1. La Reina. Security Trust and Savings Bank. Los Angeles. 1929. p. 39.
8. Altman, James David. *Mr. Lincoln's War on the South*. James David Altman. Charleston. n.d. pp. 3-10.
9. Gilbert, Benjamin F. "The Mythical Johnston Conspiracy." *California Historical Society Quarterly*. Vol. 28. N° 2. June, 1949. p. 165.
10. Hill, p. 39.
11. McGroarty, John Steven. *History of Los Angeles*. Vol. I. of *History of Los Angeles County*. American Historical Society, Inc. Chicago. 1923. pp. 185, 303, 306.
12. Spalding, William A. *History and Reminiscences: Los Angeles City and County, California*. J. R. Finnell & Sons Publishing Company. Los Angeles. 1930. Vol. I. p. 163.
13. Gilbert, pp. 165-171.
14. Roland, Charles P. *Albert Sidney Johnston: Soldier of Three Republics*. University of Texas Press. Austin. 1964. pp. 241-242.
15. Roland, pp. 241-242.
16. Roland, p. 244.
17. Josephy, Alvin M., Jr. *The Civil War in the American West*. Alfred A. Knopf. New York. 1991. pp. 231-236.
18. United States War Department. *The War of the Rebellion: A Compilation of the Official Records of the Union and Confederate Armies*. Series I. Vol. L. Pt. l. pp. 444-446, 453.
19. O. R. Series I. Vol. L. Pt. 1. pp. 477-451.

20. *O. R.* Series I. Vol. L. Pt. 1. pp. 456-468.
21. <u>*O. R.*</u> Series I. Vol. L. Pt. 1. pp. 448.
22. Gilbert, p. 166.
23. Roland, pp. 245-247.
24. *O. R.* Series I. Vol. L. Pt. 1. pp. 455-456.
25. Gilbert, p. 170.
26. Josephy, pp. 235-236.0. R. Series I. Vol. L. Pt. 1. pp. 463.464.
27. *O. R.* Series I. Vol. L. Pt. 1. p. 496 ..
28. *O. R.* Series I. Vol. L. Pt. l. pp. 471-472.
29. Roland, pp. 249-253.Gilbert, 165-171.
30. Johnston, William Preston. *The Life of General Albert Sidney Johnston*. Da Capo Press. New York. 1997. pp. 257-276.0. R. Series I. Vol. L. Pt: 1. p. 496.
31. *O. R.* Series I. Vol. L. Pt. 1. p. 496.
32. Johnston, p. 277.
33. Armistead, Gene. "California's Confederate Militia: The Los Angeles Mounted Rifles." *Confederate Veteran*. Vol. 3. 1997.pp. 19-20.
34. Armistead, p. 20.
35. Johnston, p. 277.
36. Johnston, p. 277. Armistead, p. 21.
37. Johnston, p. 278.Armistead, p. 21.
38. Armistead, pp. 21-22.
39. Johnston, pp. 279-280.Armistead, p. 22.
40. Johnston, p. 281.Armistead, p. 23.
41. Johnston, p. 281.Armistead, pp. 23-24.
42. *O. R.* Series I. Vol. L.Pt. 1. p. 566.
43. Hioleman, Mary B. "Crossed the Plains With Johnston." *Confederate Veteran*. Vol. 3. 1995.p. 333.
44. Colton, Ray C. *The Civil War in the Western Territories*. University of Oklahoma Press. Norman. 1959.p. 19.
45. *O. R.* Series I. Vol. IV. pp. 17-20.
46. Johnston, 289. Armistead, p. 28.
47. Johnston, p. 281. Armistead, pp: 22, 25.
48. Armistead, p. 18.
49. Kerby, Robert Lee. T*he Confederate Invasion of New Mexico and Arizona, 1861-1862*. Westernlore Press. Los Angeles. 1958. p. 40.
50. *O. R.* Series I. Vol. L. Pt. 1. p. 639.
51. *O. R.* Series I. Vol. L. Pt. 1. pp. 628-630.
52. Kibby, Leo P. "California, The Civil War, and the Indian Problem: an Account of California's Participation in the Great Conflict." *Journal of the*

West. N°. 4 1965. p. ·40,

53. Gilbert, p. 171.Armistead, p. 28. Johnston, p. 277.

54. Kibby, p. 297.

55. Bancroft, Hubert Howe. *The Works of Hubert Howe Bancroft*. Vol. VII. *History of California, 1860-1890*. The History Company Publishers. San Francisco. 1890. p. 282. Armistead, 28.

News of the arrival of the Californians at Mesilla.

CHAPTER III. JOSEPH LANCASTER BRENT.

Joseph Lancaster Brent, a native of Maryland, was as much a Californian as a North American could become; he was an attorney who was widely respected by both his Anglo peers and his California friends. He was a leader in activities in the Democratic Party of Los Angeles, and, as were most lawyers of Southern heritage in Los Angeles, sympathetic to the Southern Cause.[1]

Brent arrived at Los Angeles in 1850, with his library of law books, and many books of general interest;[2] he had left his first Californian residence at San Francisco to practice law in Los Angeles. Brent's law books, very scarce in California, came from the library of his father, Congressman William Leigh Brent.[3]

He was admitted to the practice of law in California on January 3, 1853, although he had begun immediately upon his arrival. Many lawyers of Los Angeles began to practice law as soon as they were able to find clients, and customarily did not wait to be admitted to the bar.[4]

Brent had an advantage over other lawyers of Los Angeles: he spoke Spanish, and had a thorough knowledge of the law of Louisiana, which is similar to the Spanish law of California. Lawyer Brent went by the name, "Lancaster," but was soon called "Don Jose" by the Californios. The young Baltimore lawyer was tall and thin, with a prominent nose, dark hair thinning at the top and long behind, smooth cheeks, drooping mustaches with a square-cut beard, keen black eyes, and the manner of a Southern gentleman. He was a direct descendant of George Calvert, the first Lord Baltimore, and must have fit well with Old California society.[5]

Brent was an able lawyer and astute politician, and was considered to be one of California's most brilliant men. He was employed by many rancheros to prove their titles; the prominent Californios placed full confidence in him, and, in their behalf, he went before the United States Land Commission. He also appeared before the United States Court of Appeals. In 1859, he triumphantly brought back from Washington the first United States patent for Los Angeles County land, dated December 18, 1858, which covered the Rancho San Pedro of Manuel Dominguez. Brent had been engaged by the City of Los Angeles on October 26, 1852, to prove the city's claim to land under the Land Act of 1851. A need to prove the claim was necessary because the city's title, like that of the ranchos, originated in the period preceding the transfer of California to the United States.[6] Brent won confirmation of the title concerning an area surveyed as 17,172 acres.[7]

J. Lancaster Brent was, indeed, a worthy counsel in the defence of Californio land claims when California became part of the United States, and holders of Spanish and Mexican land grants were obliged to defend what was theirs. Brent became an expert in land titles. Once, when he was in San Francisco on business before the Land Commission, he became a friend of California's United States Senator, William Gwin; Senator Gain was the author of the California Land Bill which had been designed to settle claims of land for both Californios and North American settlers.[8] Their collaboration would play a significant role in later years.

Brent associated with such early Californians as the Carillos, Figueroas, Zamoranos, David Alexander, the Pimientos, Henry Dalton, the de la Peñas, Alexander P. Crittenden, the Alvarados, the Griffins (Albert Sidney Johnston's in-laws), the Verdugos, the del Valles, the Varellas, and other prominent people of early California who were lawyers, politicians, and agriculturists.[9] During a legal action which drew much public attention, Brent successfully defended the claim of the "Scotch Paisano" Hugo Reid to the Mission San Gabriel; in 1852, as a token of his appreciation, Reid willed his large library to Brent.[10]

Brent's legal work was not confined to matters of land title; a famous case involved his defence of four young men of the Lugo family on the charge of murder. On November 12, 1851, the Lugo party, in pursuit of horse thieves, were directed into an ambush by an Indian, which resulted in several fatalities. The four Lugos avenged their loss by the killing of an Indian in the Cajon Pass. Brent was successful in getting the Lugos acquitted,[11] and was paid $20,000 for his work.[12] In another criminal trial, William Lee was being tried for murder. Brent, the defence attorney, and Benjamin Hays, the prosecuting attorney, found that the case led to "an interruption of all personal intercourse" between Hays, Brent, and "another counsel in that case."[13]

J. Lancaster Brent also performed public service willingly, served as president of the first Los Angeles School Board,[14] and was a School Commissioner in 1853.[15]

In the 1850s, several members of the legal profession of Los Angeles served with the Rangers, a semi-vigilante body of men organized in 1853 at the El Dorado Saloon, having the purpose of lowering crime in a city filled with criminals; there were a hundred or more men in the organization, who regarded themselves as a "law and order" group. The Rangers were credited with twenty-two executions of criminals in 1854 and 1855. J. Lancaster Brent was a Ranger,[16] as were many other prominent citizens of Los Angeles; other units of volunteer police were formed at about the same time.

One of Brent's Ranger comrades was the notorious Roy Bean, who went from Los Angeles to New Mexico during the War to help organize a company of Confederate volunteers; after the war, Bean settled at what became Langtree, Texas, a railway station just west of the Pecos River, named for the celebrated actress, where he opened the Jersey Lily Saloon, and became Justice of the Peace. He held court in the saloon, and took jurisdiction of every case brought before him in the manner of a Californian alcalde. "Judge" Roy Bean became famous throughout the United States as "The Law West of the Pecos."[17]

Brent later enlisted as a private of the "Southern-oriented" Los Angeles Mounted Rifles who escorted General Johnston into Confederate Arizona Territory, and appears on the first and only muster of the Rifles, dated March 7, 1861.[18] He was not a part of that escort of June and July, 1861, but waited until October, 1861, to leave California by sea.

Ignacio del Valle, the descendant of a Spanish family which had been settled in California since the 1700s, let law offices to Brent, and became his close friend.[19] Senor del Valle and his wife Ysabel Varella, the daughter of a prominent California family, owned Rancho San Francisco in the area of Castaic; their home at Comulos inspired Helen Hunt Jackson, in the latter part of the century, to write *Ramona*,[20] the famous novel depicting the ruin of the Californian Indians. The strong friendship between Brent and the del Valles led Brent to assume the duties and responsibilities of a godfather to the twelve children of Ignacio and Ysabel. Six of Ysabel's sons would be named Jose in his honour.[21]

Brent became a southern Californian landowner in the manner his California friends; the Marengo Tract of 800 acres, partly in Pasadena and partly in South Pasadena, was originally purchased in 1855 by Brent from Don Manuel Garafias. Brent's favourite hero was Napoleon Bonaparte, and he named the ranch after the Napoleonic battlefield of Marengo.[22] Brent, together with J. D. Hunter and J. R. Scott, bought the land that inspired the creation of the city of Burbank.[23]

Brent was active in the organization of the Democratic Party in California; his influence was such that he brought many Californios to support the party's causes. He taught Don Julio Verdugo and his sons, who were co-owners of the Rancho San Rafael, how to vote the straight Democratic ticket.[24] In 1853, the Burbank Verdugos, Julio and his thirteen sons, were led to the polls to vote for the candidate favoured by the Verdugo's attorney, Joseph Lancaster Brent; the sons always accompanied their father on election day. On those occasions, Brent, whose political influence with the old man was supreme, distributed, through the father, fourteen election tickets containing the names of his favoured candidates.[25] It was said Brent could nominate any candidate at will; he himself twice served in the California Legislature,[26] and also as City Attorney of Los Angeles. Brent's office in del Valle's hall soon became a rallying point for the Democrats of Los Angeles.[27]

The Republican victory of 1860, the subsequent secession of the Southern states, and the birth in 1861 of the Confederate States of America, caused Joseph Lancaster Brent to leave the good life he had in Los Angeles. Like most lawyers of the city, Brent's sympathies were strongly with the South, and, accordingly, Brent began his journey to join the Confederacy in mid-October, 1861, at San Diego,[28] where he joined former Senator William Gwin and former United States Attorney and Californian state legislator, Calhoun Benham, on board of the steamship *Orazaba* bound for Panama; the three agreed to occupy quarters together.

General Sumner, who, together with his staff, had been recalled from California to the war in the east, were also aboard the *Orazaba*. There were rumours aboard that Gwin and his companions were bound for the Confederacy; some said that members of Sumner's staff had been approached by one or more of the three Southerners with an offer of a commission in the Confederate Army. Another passenger of strong Southern sympathy on the *Orazaba* was Lillie Hitchcock, the daughter of Dr. Charles Hitchcock, a native of Maryland, who was a physician of San Francisco, and Martha Hunter Hitchcock, who was born and raised on a plantation in North Carolina. The Hitchcock family had come to San Francisco in 1851 when the doctor, an army surgeon, was assigned there.

When the Confederacy came into being, a wide rift erupted in the Hitchcock family; Charles Hitchcock, a graduate of West Point and friend of Jefferson Davis, was offered the position of Medical Director of the Confederate Army. However fond the doctor was of the South, he believed the South could not possibly win against the Federal government, and took Lillie to task for being a rebel; Lillie considered her father a defector. She was warned by her father not to express her sympathies, because those who expressed support for the Southern cause in San Francisco found themselves in serious trouble; soon, the wives of San Francisco's Southerners who insisted upon expressing their views were sent to Paris to await the war's end. Lillie and her mother, Martha, were amongst them, and hence Lillie's presence aboard the *Orazaba*, bound for the East Coast by way of the Isthmus of Panama.

Lillie, who knew most prominent Californians socially, had met Brent, and knew he was a former Marylander and a Southern patriot; she was an old friend of Gwin and Benham in San Francisco. As Lillie enjoyed a conversation with her three friends, Gwin and Benham were summoned to meet with General Sumner. After they departed, Brent confided to Lillie he believed Sumner would take Gwin and Benham prisoner. She inquired if either of them were carrying documents to the Confederacy, for she was convinced her friends were part of an effort to take California out of the Union.

Brent informed her there existed such papers, but they were now in his possession. He was concerned that, because of his traveling companions, he, too, would come under suspicion, and thus the papers would be discovered; Lillie requested him to give her the papers, and promised she would make certain that they would be carried to the proper officials of the Confederacy. After some hesitation, Brent gave her the papers in a sealed packet, telling her that they contained maps of military installations in California, and intelligence about mining operations.[29] Sumner placed Gwin, Benham, and Brent under arrest for having a Southern destination, conscious "that they were active Democrats and enemies of the government." The arrests were made in the Gulf of Panama. Gwin, Benham, and Brent went voluntarily across the Isthmus and on to New York with Sumner in order to prevent armed conflict between U. S. and Columbian forces, for Columbia had challenged the authority of Sumner to make arrests on Columbian territory. Sumner called upon a U. S. warship which was in the Gulf for aid, at which point the three arrested men volunteered to accompany him to avoid an incident.[30]

Sumner and his prisoners arrived at New York on November 15, 1861, on the steamer *Champion*; Sumner released Brent, Benham, and Gwin on parole, but an order from William Seward was given to imprison the three men at Fort Lafayette. While they were confined there, influential friends of the three attempted to get them released, and, in the end, found it necessary to go over Seward's head to the president with the claim the men had received a legal safe conduct from Sumner, who had then performed an illegal arrest on foreign territory. Lincoln freed the men who, after a hearing, were released unconditionally; both Benham and Brent went south and joined the Confederacy.[31]

Lillie and her mother were able to disembark without interference; although their sympathies were known to General Sumner, Brent's packet got through. Lillie had hid it in her dirty laundry bag. Martha and Lillie made their way across the Isthmus and up the East Coast to New York with the other passengers of the *Orazaba*, including the arrested Gwin, Benham, and Brent.

Before crossing the Atlantic to Paris, the Hitchcock ladies took advantage of the less-than-full Northern blockade of Southern ports at that time, and inspected some family property in Georgia. Lillie lost no time in riding to nearby Darian and the Confederate training camp just beyond, where she delivered Brent's papers to the field commander, who expressed gratitude for their delivery: there seems to be no further information regarding if or how that information was used by the Confederacy.

After the war, Lillie returned to San Francisco and married Howard Coit; her estate donated the landmark, Coit Tower, which stands atop Telegraph Hill.[32]

Brent offered his services to the Confederacy in the winter of 1861, and served as Brigadier General John B. Magruder's chief of ordnance during the Peninsular Campaign in Virginia, although he had no formal military training; later, he-served as Major General Richard Taylor's chief of artillery and ordnance in the Trans-Mississippi Department, where Brent commanded the small expedition that captured the Federal ironclad *Indianola* during the Vicksburg campaign. Taylor was impressed with Brent's energy and administrative ability,[33] owing to which distinction Brent became a brigadier general.[34]

While serving in the Trans-Mississippi Department, Brent wrote the only known battle report which directly discusses the activities and casualties of the Confederate artillery at Mansfield and Pleasant Hill, Louisiana, which resulted in disaster for an ambitious Union effort to capture the headquarters of the Trans-Mississippi Department at Shreveport, Louisiana, and invade Texas. A Confederate army inflicted heavy casualties and routed the Unionists on April 8, 1864, at Mansfield; the next day, at Pleasant Hill, the Union army were again defeated. Brent, who commanded the artillery during the battle, documented the position and activities of each participating battery at the two battles, including casualties and losses of equipment; his report is the only one available to historians.[35]

The editor of the *Los Angeles Star* appeared to be quite proud of the citizens of Los Angeles fighting for the Confederacy; some who were frequently mentioned were Alonzo Ridley, with General Forest's cavalry; George W. Gift, lieutenant in the Confederate Navy who saw action on the Mississippi River: and Joseph Lancaster Brent, when he was chief of ordinance for General Magruder.[36]

The brother of Ysabel Varella del Valle, Antonio Varella, was with the Confederate forces commanded by his fellow Angeleno, Albert Sidney Johnston; to quiet her fears about Antonio's safe return, she paid for the oil to keep a flame alive in his name before the image of the Blessed Virgin in the Old Plaza Church. When Brent left to fight for the South, Ysabel feared for her children's godfather as well, and, as soon as Ignacio had built her a chapel, she planned to light a flame of intercession for both of them. Ignacio and Ysabel must have followed Brent's adventures with anxious interest through newspaper accounts of the War. When he had been released at New York, Brent was commissioned a major in the Confederate Army at New Orleans; he was named a colonel in the field in April, 1864, and, six months later, a brigadier general. He was one of the last three Confederate generals who surrendered the tattered remnants of their armies;[37] the other two were Sterling Price and Simon Bolivar Bruckner. The army they surrendered to E. R. S. Canby at New Orleans in May, 1865, was that of E. Kirby Smith.[38]

After the surrender, Brent chose to remain at New Orleans, where he married Rosella Kenner, the daughter of a confidant of Jefferson Davis and a Louisianan legislator. Brent was elected to that legislature, and pursued a long and distinguished political career in Louisiana and in his native Maryland. Saddened by the knowledge that Brent would not return to Los Angeles, Ysabel del Valle prepared to keep her vow to light a lamp in her chapel in gratitude to God for sparing Don Jose's life and that of her brother, Antonio. Brent remained in communication with his Californian friends by letter, and continued his land business there.[39] Harris Nemark, author of *Sixty Years in Southern California: 1853-1913*, met Brent again whilst attending the Centennial Exposition in 1876.[40] In 1885, Brent, now called "General" for his Confederate service, bought a 671-acre portion of the Rancho San Rafael along the Los Angeles River.[41]

General Joseph Lancaster Brent died at Baltimore, Maryland, on November 27, 1905. Surviving him was his widow; a son, Duncan Kenner Brent: and a daughter, Nanine Brent. His obituary stated, "Brent's broad views and high standards of right made him an effective worker in the real reconstruction of the South."[42]

One spring morning in 1874, the del Valles were visited by Ysabel's brother, Antonio Varella, who was accompanied by Alonzo Ridley, who had left the Confederate service as a colonel. Both Antonio and Brent had served under Ridley, the same former Captain Ridley of the Los Angeles Mounted Rifles who had escorted Albert Sidney Johnston out of California. Ridley had been trained as a Confederate structural engineer, and was so embittered when Brent was forced to surrender in May, 1865, that he refused to take the oath of allegiance to his enemies from the north, and fled to Mexico. While in Mexico, Ridley worked as an engineer for the Emperor Maximilian until Maximilian's murder in June, 1867. Ridley built railways and bridges for the new Mexican government, and remained there; his daughter lived at the del Valles's home, and received letters from him there. He continued his visits to the del Valles throughout his life, but never established residence again in a California governed by the Yankees from Washington.[43]

NOTES TO CHAPTER III.

1. Robinson, W. W. *Lawyers of Los Angeles Bar Association and the Bar of Los Angeles County*. Los Angeles Bar Association. Los Angeles. 1959. p. 37.
2. McGroarty, Vol. I. pp. 73, 104.
3. Smith, Wallace E. *This Land Was Ours: the del Valles and Camulos*. Ed. Grant W. Heil. Ventura County Historical Society. Ventura. 1977. pp. 78-79.
4. W. W., Robinson, pp. 33-34.
5. Smith, pp. 78-79.
6. W. W., Robinson, pp. 34-35.
7. Brent was a pioneer in the law of land title in California; the first Los Angeles title was confirmed through Brent's work is recorded in Land Commission Case 422, United States District Court, Case N°. 366, Southern Division. Most Los Angeles County patents were issued in the 1870s. W. W. Robinson, p. 35.
8. Smith, p. 91.
9. Smith, pp. 90-100.
10. Smith, p. 79.
11. Hayes, Benjamin. *Pioneer Notes From the Diaries of Judge Benjamin Hayes*, 1849-1875. Marjorie Tisdale Wolcott. Los Angeles. 1929. p. 75.
12. Smith, p. 78.
13. Hayes, p. 187.
14. Hill, Laurence L. *La Reina*. Security Trust and Savings Bank. Los Angeles. 1929. p. 39.
15. W. W. Robinson. p. 227.
16. W. W. Robinson, p. 225.
17. W. M. Robinson, p. 42.
18. Muster Roll of the Los Angeles Mounted Rifles. California Militia Document. Los Angeles. March 7, 186. p. 2.
19. Smith, p. 79.
20. Charles H. Heil. Letter to Laurence F. Talbott. 23 September 1994. Ventura, California.

21. Smith, p. 84.
22. Carew, Harold E. *History of Pasadena and the San Gabriel Valley, California*. The S. J. Clarke Publishing Company. Sierra Madre. 1930. p. 319.
23. Mayers, Jackson. Burbank History. James W. Anderson. Burbank. 1975.
24. W. W. Robinson, p. 36.
25. Mayers, pp. 16-17.
26. W. W. Robinson, pp. 36.
27. Smith, p. 79.
28. W. W. Robinson, p. 37.
29. Holdridge, Helen. *Firebelle Lillie*. Meridith Press. New York.1967. pp. 2, 12, 33-38, 135-150.
30. Thomas, Lately. *Between Two Empires*. Houghton Mifflin Company. Boston. 1969. pp. 265-267.
31. Thomas, pp. 271-272.
32. Holdridge, pp. 151-153, 295.
33. Johansson, Jane Harris, and David R. Johansson. "Two 'Lost' Battle Reports: Horace Randal's and Joseph L. Brent's Reports of the Battles of Mansfield and Pleasant Hill, 8 and 9 April, 1864." *Military History of the West*. Vol.23, N° 22. Autumn, 1993. p. 176.
34. *Illustrated History of Los Angeles County*. The Lewis Publishing Company. Chicago. 1889. p. 161.
35. Johansson, pp. 169-171.
36. Robinson, John W. *Los Angeles in Civil War Days, 1860-65*. Dawson's Bookshop. Los Angeles. 1977. p. 112.
37. Smith, pp. 121-122.
38. *Illustrated History of Los Angeles County*. p. 161.
39. Smith, p. 123.
40. Newmark, Harris. *Sixty Years in Southern California, 1853-1913*. The Knickerbocker Press. New York. 1916. p. 295.
41. Mayers, p. 22.
42. *California Scrapbook, Los Angeles*. Los Angeles Public Library. n. d. Vol. 2, Pt. 1.
43. Smith, pp. 163-164.

CHAPTER IV. CAMERON ERSKINE THOM.

Cameron Erskine Thom was born into an aristocratic Scotch family of Culpepper, Virginia, in 1825; after migrating from Scotland, the family continued to be part of the aristocracy, in both social standing and way of life, of Virginia. Thom's father had been a soldier in the War of Revolution, later a high sheriff, and then a senator for Virginia in the United States Congress.[1]

Thom was an active, adventurous young man, who went to California in the Gold Rush of 1849; he chose to make the overland trip to the goldfields in preference to that of the sea.[2] He left Virginia in grand style, with about thirty other young men mounted on fine horses, their possessions loaded in waggons; included in the cavalcade was a cook's waggon with eight black cooks to ensure them a diet of good Southern cuisine. On the way to California, Thom's party encountered the Sioux, and immediately made friends with them; they lived in the homes of the Sioux for six weeks, thoroughly enjoying the Indian way of life, and, apparently, the Sioux enjoyed the company of the high-spirited young Virginians who parted from them in peace and with good will.

After the party had arrived at Sacramento, the members went their own ways, the majority of them going to Rose Bar, near Marysville, where most of them died of typhoid fever; there seems to be no record of the fate of the eight cooks.[3] Thom engaged in mining in northern California, where areas of his attempts at mining included the South Fork of the American River, and Mormon Island.[4] After three years of hard work, with little or no success, he abandoned any hope of striking it rich, and, in 1853, decided to practice law, the profession for which he was educated. The law was a prosperous business in California.

In the course of his law practice, Thom had the need to travel to Marysville; there he met and married Susan Henrietta Hathwell, the daughter of one of the best-known physicians of the region. In the 1850s, there was much litigation over land titles, so Thom, like Brent, became involved in land claims, and was eventually appointed the San Francisco Agent of the United States Land Commission.[5] In 1854, one of his assignments took him to Los Angeles;[6] when he had finished his work there, and was scheduled to be transferred to another city, he found he did not want to leave. It was a fortunate choice.[7]

Thom brought his practice to Los Angeles, and became one of the most distinguished men of his day.[8] He was a brilliant lawyer, and, two years after his arrival, he was elected to the post of City Attorney and

County Attorney at the same time. Election to those two offices resulted in his having to defend both sides in a land dispute between the city and the county.[9] He was re-elected and served three terms. In 1856, he was elected to the Legislature.[10]

During the War for Southern Independence, Unionists were a minority at Los Angeles; most of the lawyers with roots in the Southern states left the city to serve in the Confederate Army;[11] like many other Angeleno lawyers, Cameron Thom served as a officer in the Confederate Army.[12] He was an ardent Southerner, and felt a sacred obligation to defend his beliefs when the war began. His exact date of departure from Los Angeles is apparently unrecorded; it is known he was still at Los Angeles about June 14, 1861, because the June 15, 1861, number of the *Los Angeles Star* carried a story about Governor Downey's visit to his home town of Los Angeles, and how he was welcomed at the Bella Union Hotel with a speech by Cameron E. Thom. The *Star* stated: "The Honourable Cameron E. Thom made a brief speech of welcome, and was followed by the Governor, who discussed current issues, declaring he was a Union man, &c."[13]

Thom left his young wife at Los Angeles, but she returned to her family at Marysville to await his return. In 1862, she became ill, and died on August 16 of that year; she was buried there in the Old City Cemetery. Thom fought through the whole war, taking part in fifteen battles, being wounded twice; he gained a reputation for valour, and, at the war's end, he held the rank of captain,[14] and little else. His country was beaten, his cause was lost, his beautiful home at Los Angeles was gone, and, worst of all, his beloved wife was dead. When his ship arrived at San Pedro, California, late in 1865, he was tired, impoverished, and heartbroken; he did not even seek old friends who had been his recent enemies.

Shortly after Thom's return to Los Angeles, he was recognised by J. M. Griffith, formerly of Marysville and Sacramento, a Republican and strong Union man, who had at one time been associated with the Big Four at Sacramento: Huntington, Crocker, Stanford, and Hopkins. In 1865, he was engaged in the transportation industry of Los Angeles. Griffith grabbed Thom by the hand, and bellowed, "Well, you dirty old rebel! You are back here now, and, if you behave yourself, we won't hang you." He then insisted on helping his old friend get back on his feet with a loan of $300 in gold, and the admonition, "Go get your hair cut, and get some clean clothes." Proud man that he was, Thom accepted the loan, for he knew the spirit in which it was offered.

Thom had one more problem to overcome before he could earn a living in his profession: one side of Northern vengeance against Southern patriots was that lawyers who had served as Confederate soldiers were disbarred, but Thom's former enemies, the Los Angeles lawyers who had supported the Union, rallied to his aid, and induced President Andrew Johnson to parole him. Heartened by this show of kindness and support, he picked up the pieces of his life, and started to rebuild his career;[15] he renewed his law practice at Los Angeles, and held public office as a state senator, later becoming mayor of Los Angeles.

Thom invested in Rancho San Rafael real estate, and, with other pioneers, pooled his acreage to establish the town site which became Glendale.

Other Confederate veterans joined Thom in Southern California. Thom's nephew, Erskine M. Ross, a Confederate veteran, came to Los Angeles in 1868, where he studied law with his uncle, was admitted to the bar the following year, became a partner with his uncle, and was a charter member of the Los Angeles Bar Association. In 1879, Ross was elected to be Justice of the Supreme Court of California. Colonel George H. Smith, a former Confederate Anny officer, came to Los Angeles, and established the law firm of Glessell, Chapman, and Smith. Glessell, Chapman, and Thom shared ownership of a portion of Rancho San Rafael which became Glendale.[16] About 1873; Thom owned, in addition to the San Rafael property of about 3,000 acres, other landholdings of approximately 50 acres.[17] Captain Thom's post-war recovery was complete when he married Belle Hathwell, his former wife's younger sister, who had grown up to be much like Susan Henrietta. Cameron and Belle Thom had three sons, all of whom prospered at Los Angeles.

From 1850 to 1870, Los Angeles was probably the toughest pioneer town in the United States. On October 24, 1871, Cameron Thom showed his integrity and courage. The marshal was killed by a wild shot during a Chinese tong war; his death inspired howling mobs who took to the streets, each mob hunting down Chinese and hanging them, men, women, and children, from telegraph poles; the mobs set fire to Chinese homes and businesses after robbing them. The sheriff tried to restore order, but without success, until Cameron Thom and Judge Whidley, head of the Law and Order League, came to the aid of the sheriff. Each man carried a loaded and cocked revolver, and each was known to be fearless. One by one, they confronted the armed mobs as they dragged their victims to the telegraph poles, and made the mobs drop the Chinese, and disperse.[18]

It was in 1883 that Thom was elected mayor of Los Angeles for the term from 1883 through 1884.[19] As time went by, Thom became a very wealthy man who owned much land, a ranch, and a fine mansion in Los

Angeles; he lived to be almost 90, dying in 1915 at that home; to the very end, he was active mentally and a busy citizen. His funeral was attended by the powerful of southern California, including judges, senators, mayors, bankers, and old friends who had held positions of great responsibility, and he was buried at Los Angeles. A biographer, Stephen G. Hust, commented, "He did all right for an ex-rebel."[20]

NOTES TO CHAPTER IV.

1. Hust, Stephen G. *This Is My Own Native Land*. Ind. Press. Yuba City. 1956. p. 89.
2. McGroarty, J. S. *History of Los Angeles*. Vol. III. of History of Los Angeles County. Am. Hist. Soc. Chicago. 1923. p. 401.
3. Hust, p. 89.
4. McGroarty, Vol. III., p. 40l.
5. Hust, p. 90.
6. McGroarty. Vol. I., p. 73.
7. Hust, p. 90.
8. McGroarty, Vol. III., p. 401.
9. Robinson, W. W. *Lawyers of Los Angeles: Hist. of L. A. Bar Assn. & Bar of L. A Cnty*. L. A. Bar Assn. L. A. 1959. p: 45.
10. Hust, p. 91.
11. W. W. Robinson, pp. 48-49.
12. W. W. Robinson, p. 46.
13. "First Hotel of Old Los Angeles." *Southern California Quarterly*. Vol. 33, N°.2. 1951. pp. 163-164.
14. Hust, p. 91. McGroarty, V. III., p. 401, calls Thom a major.
15. Hust, p. 91.
16. W. W. Robinson, pp. 46-49.
17. McGroarty, Vol. III., p. 401.
18. Hust, p. 92.
19. Spalding, Wm. *A History and Reminiscences: Los Angeles City and County, California*. J. R. Finnell & Sons Puhl. Co. Los Angeles. 1930. Vol. I. pp. 248-251.
20. Hust, p. 92.

CHAPTER V. JUDGES DAVID S. TERRY AND LANGFORD W. HASTINGS.

The life of David S. Terry, Chief Justice of the California Supreme Court, was one of spectacular adventure, success, and tragedy. Terry was born in Kentucky on March 8, 1823; his ancestors had migrated to America before the Revolution, and were, for the most part, prosperous Virginia and Carolina planters. Both of his grandfathers were patriot officers in the Revolutionary War who later removed across the Appalachians. Terry's branch of the family went to Texas in 1833 or early 1834; Terry claimed he had fought for Texan independence at the age of about 13. He never returned to formal education after the Texas Revolution, saying that he refused to go from soldier to schoolboy.[1] During the Mexican War, Terry joined the Texas Rangers, already a famous fighting unit, and served as a private soldier; little, therefore, is known of his deeds other than the information in his service record, which mentions that he participated in the battle of Monterrey, and there engaged in door-to-door street fighting.

It is impossible truly to understand David S. Terry's personality and philosophy of life without considering his Texan origins, of which his experience as a Ranger was an important part. The Rangers and men of South Texas were hard-living men; Terry had fought in two wars, and was a member of a frontier society, accustomed to living with vigorous, rough men. The intense Southern sympathies were his throughout his life came from his background, birthplace, and early training; his character had come down to him from his ancestors.[2] Terry studied law in the office of T. B. J. Hadley, his uncle, and, in 1845, took the bar examination; his legal experience in Texas was also valuable in California, for, on the frontier, knowledge of the law was secondary to an ability to deal with rough courtroom procedure.

Early in 1849, David S. Terry joined the Gold Rush to California;[3] he later settled at Stockton, practiced law, and engaged in local operations of the Democratic Party. He left the Democratic Party in 1855 to join the American or "Know Nothing" Party, and was elected a Justice of the California Supreme Court on that party's ticket, winning, in part, because he had built a solid reputation as a Californian lawyer.[4]

Whilst in the Democratic Party as a "Chivalry Democrat," Terry was nominated by those Southern Democrats for Chief Justice of the California Supreme Court; the nomination came after the split of the Democratic

Laurence F. Talbott, PhD

Party at their 1857 Convention over differences regarding the nomination of candidates for the 1860 election. In California, the Northern Democrats sought to nominate the United States Senator, David C. Broderick, as a Californian senator, but were soundly defeated by Senator William M. Gwin of the "Chivalry Democrats." Terry had, from the beginning of the party split, given his allegiance to the "Chivalry" faction.

Although Terry was intensely Southern, as were his principles and sympathies in political matters, he was not, nor had he ever been, a supporter or personal friend of Gwin, who was Broderick's political foe. There existed between Terry and Broderick a fair, if not warm, degree of personal admiration, of Terry for incorruptible integrity as a public officer, arid of Broderick for his determination and courage; during the particularly vitriolic election, however, Judge Terry made some remarks which irritated Broderick. Then, on June 26, 1857, Broderick burst forth in public, with a tirade which included calling Terry, then Chief Justice of the State Supreme Court, "the damned miserable wretch."[5]

The election occurred on September 7, 1857, with a sweeping defeat of the Northern Democrats and Republicans.

The aftermath of the election was bitter indeed for Broderick, who had been nominated, but now had but two months left to serve. Terry demanded an apology for Broderick's attack on his character, initiating an exchange of notes. A simple, dignified apology from Broderick might have avoided the affair that ended in a duel. Chief Justice Terry felt deeply offended by the language Senator Broderick had used, whose insults had been published across the state, and thus were common talk. Judge Terry sought only the retraction of the offensive language as words used in an impulsive moment under temporary passion. Some of Broderick's moderate friends insisted Terry's request was fair and proper, no more than Broderick himself would expect if the situation had been reversed, and advised that, with mutual assurances of former respect and good feelings, past friendly relations would be restored; other associates of more aggressive nature, however, had more influence over Broderick, who refused any accomodation.[6]

Broderick's aggressive associates had a twofold reason for pushing the affair to an inevitable, violent conclusion; it was well known that Senator Broderick had become, by assiduous and skilled training, one of the most capable men in California at the use of a pistol. He could shoot with surprising accuracy, and with the unusual ability to recognise his target at a single glance. There was riot a man who could equal Broderick, if challenged, in quick and accurate pistol fire, it was thought by those who knew him. They felt confident in his fierce courage and in his emerging victorious in any hostile encounter. The second reason some of Broderick's associates wanted violence was to prove to the "Chivalry" faction that Broderick, as an acknowledged chief and "boldest champion of the Northern element" was as ready to fight as the bravest Southern leaders; they also knew Terry, although an experienced soldier with a rifle, was not expert in the use of pistols, and had never participated in a duel: indeed, he had witnessed only one in the course of his life.[7]

Terry made an apparent attempt to refrain from pressing his differences with Broderick to a violent conclusion; his note would have allowed Broderick to close the correspondence, and lead to a mutual friendly explanation and renewed amicable relations, but Broderick's advisors, who wanted a duel, prevailed. Broderick's notes left Terry no alternatives except to withdraw his justified demand, which would have been viewed as cowardly, or challenge Broderick to a duel: such was the culture of California at that time, and, accordingly, Terry became the challenger. Broderick could not both retreat with honour, and save himself from the charge of cowardice.

A former New Yorker, Colonel Thomas Hays, one of Broderick's earliest supporters at San Francisco, and David Colton of Siskiyou, assisted Broderick; Colonel Calhoun Benham assisted Terry as second. The conditions of the duel were that, after each participant said he was ready, the word "fire" would be given, followed by the words "one" and "two;" neither man was to raise his pistol before the word "fire," or shoot before the word "two." Terry's second objected to the site selected for the meeting and the unprecedented brevity of the firing time, because the short time was contrary to the custom of California; the choice of weapons and conditions, however, were the right of the challenged party. Terry waived objections to the conditions, believing it might appear as if he were seeking a pretext to back out of an affair which he was expected to lose because of Broderick's superior skill and speed.[8]

When other last-minute attempts to defuse the situation were made by prominent San Franciscans, they were told by Broderick's cortege, "It is no use. You are too late. The fight has got to come, and this is the best time for it. Broderick never had a better chance, and he isn't going to get hurt. He can bit the size of a ten-cent piece at this distance every time. These 'Chivs' have got to learn there is one man they can't back down." Broderick said to his friend, John White, "Don't you fear, John. I shoot twice to Terry's once, beat him shooting every time."[9]

Laurence F. Talbott, PhD

When the duel began, at nearly 7 A. M. on the morning of Tuesday, September 10, 1859, Terry was apparently the more composed of the two; he had been made aware of Broderick's skill, and was duly conscious of his own disadvantage, especially with respect to the rapid form of aiming and firing. The duel began when both men agreed that they were ready; then came the words "fire" and "one." Almost at the word "one," Broderick fired; the ball from his pistol hit the ground before Terry, who immediately returned fire before "two," and struck Broderick in the breast. The ball pierced Broderick's lung; he died on September 16, 1859.[10]

Broderick immediately became a martyr in the San Francisco press which supported the Northern faction of the Democratic Party. The press and public outcry radically revised the causes of the duel, from a quarrel over verbal insults and intransigence between two public men fastidious about the perception of their honour, into the first shots of a sectional war; in one account, incidentally, the Southern Chief Justice was supposed to have lost. Broderick's death was supposedly for a principle, that of anti-slavery; Terry was called a murderer, even though he was not skilled at dueling, and fought under conditions every one concerned knew were to his disadvantage. Broderick's death had deeply stung the Californians of Northern sympathy who had seen their doctrines and their candidate rejected in the recent election.[11]

At the outbreak of the War, there was great concern among Union sympathisers that Terry had become, or would become, the leader of a western secessionist movement;[12] the war damaged his practice in California, and Terry, conscious of his responsibility to his family and the stringency of his financial position, may have rationalised to himself he was serving the Confederacy better in the West than he could from an eastern battlefield.[13] He traveled between California and Nevada Territory in his legal practice during 1860 and 1861, and was acknowledged to be one of the most important "Chivalry" men in Nevada.[14]

In California, the warrants for the arrest of Terry on charges of murder from his duel with Broderick still hung over him until the summer of 1860, for the matter had continued for months. Although the courts exonerated Terry, pro-Northern sentiment in California was anti-Terry, and the view he had murdered Broderick for political reasons became widespread. Terry's actions were thus described: "The man that challenged him is a dead shot, for he has killed several." This was widely believed to be true, although the facts were that Terry was untried with a pistol, had never before fought a duel, and his opponent was a noted marksman with dueling experience, who, at the moment of the duel, did actually cheat.[15]

As Terry traveled from California to make a living, the Union military were continually informed, by Union men, of Terry's alleged activity in support of the Confederacy. A few examples of correspondence will illustrate such Union communication. On May 26, 1861, a telegraph dispatch from the Committee of Safety of Virginia City, Nevada, to Captain T. Henderson, commanding officer of Fort Churchill, said the secessionists had formed an organisation of more than 100 under Dr. McMeans,[16] the goal of whom being to seize the Fort and take possession of the territory. "Judge Terry is expected soon."[17]

A dispatch from Major George A. H. Blake, Post Commander, to Major Don Carlos Buell, at Fort Churchill, dated June 5, 1861, informed Buell "there is positive information that two hundred men have organised themselves in favour of the Southern Confederacy, and have raised the Confederate flag. The men are well armed. One of their number, Dr. McMeans, late State Treasurer from California, avows he is acting under the authority of the Confederacy. It is also rumoured that Judge Terry has the commission of Governor of the territory from Jefferson Davis, and is only waiting for an opportunity to act." The dispatch ends with a request for more men and arms.

Enclosed in the dispatch of June 5 was a letter from Charles Duval to A. Briggs, Esq., which stated a group of 37 men had been formed to help Jefferson Davis take the territory, who had been enrolled by McMeans. Terry, of course, was to join them soon.[18]

A dispatch dated September 16, 1861, was sent by Jno. W. Davidson, Captain, First Cavalry, to Captain Richard C. Drum, Assistant Adjutant General, San Francisco, California, which alerted the Department of the Pacific that Judge Terry was said to be the head of a Confederate organisation which held secret nightly meetings with armed men at The Monte;[19] the area referred to as "The Monte" is El Monte, California, about twelve miles east of Los Angeles.

A dispatch dated November 4, 1861, was sent from James H. Carleton, Colonel, First California Volunteers, at his headquarters at Los Angeles, to Major Edwin A. Rigg, Commanding Officer at Camp Wright, to alert the major that Californian volunteers for the Confederate Army were attempting to pass into Arizona by the southern route taken by Johnston. The Colonel wrote: "Mr. Showalter, and men of that stripe, must be searched for expected evidence of treason. If Judge Terry tries to pass, he must go through the same ordeal. There must be no child's play with him." Major Rigg was warned to watch for little parties attempting to dodge him.[20] Carleton's concern about Terry is apparent in another communication dated November 4, 1861; he instructed a Mr. Eyre of San Francisco to confine Judge Terry at Alcatraz. In another letter to Lt. Colonel Joseph R. West, Commanding Officer of Fort Yuma, dated November 5, 1861, Carleton wrote that Judge Terry was expected to cross the desert to Arizona, and that, if Terry, when approached, showed any fight, he was to be hanged. A later dispatch to Major Rigg, dated February 25, 1862, asked, "Have you heard any rumours of Judge Terry?"[21]

It seems reasonably obvious David S. Terry had become something of a legend; he could not possibly have been at all of the places at once, or traveled through Union lines undetected. There seems concern or perhaps fear of Terry on the part of Colonel Carleton of the California Volunteers.

If it had been Terry's intention to serve the Confederacy from California, he certainly succeeded, for he was a thorn in the side of the Army of the Pacific as long as he remained in the region. He was apparently believed to be in command of Nevada's Confederate forces as Jefferson Davis' Governor of Nevada Territory, and commander of some of the Southern adherents in California; paradoxically, although Terry was a source of irritation for the military authorities, they did not wish him to leave California, as some prominent Southerners had done, to join the Confederacy.[22]

No evidence has been found in the official records of the Union and Confederate Armies, or elsewhere, to support the charges that Terry engaged in activities against the Federal government in Nevada, or that he had a commission from the Confederacy for such action; the "Governor of Nevada" rumour may be discarded, with little doubt, as fiction. On the other hand, it may be assumed Terry knew what secessionists were doing in Nevada; at the very most, Terry may have thought Nevada could be taken by force for the Confederacy. More probably, he saw in flag waving and other signs of Southern sympathy an opportunity to create tension, and, perhaps, cause a diversion of troops from California.

If so, it worked; by early June of 1861, General Sumner, the commanding officer of the Department of the Pacific, was convinced there was a secessionist threat in Nevada, and agreed to increase the garrison at Fort Churchill. If Unionist Californians were making life unpleasant for David S. Terry, he was making life uneasy for them.[23]

Rumours of Terry's actions were not confined to California and Nevada; during May, 1862, there was a Southern intelligence report that Judge Terry of California was raising 1,500 troops for Confederate service with General John R. Baylor, C. S. A., in Arizona. The news caused a slight, but short-lived, improvement of morale among Baylor's embattled troops.[24]

Terry did not officially enter the service of the Confederacy until 1863.[25] His brother, Frank, was killed in the service of the Confederacy early in the war; another brother, Clinton, who had built a promising legal practice at Brazoria, Texas, joined the Terry Texas Rangers, named after brother Frank. He was killed shortly after joining the unit when the Rangers rode into an ambush.

It seems the death of Clinton Terry was the determining force which caused the Judge to offer his services to the South in an official capacity; his exact date of departure has not been determined, because he was cautious in his preparations to leave California as it was then necessary for him to be. The capture of the Showalter party, a group on their way to the Confederacy which had followed Albert Sidney Johnston's southern route, demonstrated the difficulty of an overland journey to the East through Arizona with a party of any size; the best route seemed to be that of taking a ship to the coast of Mexico, and thence crossing overland to Texas.

Mrs. Terry and their three sons, with another child on the way, remained at Stockton. Before Terry's service with the Confederacy had ended, one son, Jefferson Davis Terry, died whilst the family were on their way to Houston; Texas, to join him, Terry boarded a vessel for Mexico early in 1863, with seven men, at least one of whom, Duncan Beaumont, was to serve under him in Texas.[26]

As Terry would have wished, confused reports of his activities continued; he was said to be carrying a brigadier general's commission with him, and to have a uniform which had been made for him in San Francisco; according to newspaper reports reaching California, Terry's party left Mazatlan on February 20, 1863. The men were experienced frontier travelers who had prepared well before starting across Mexico; as they came near the east coast, Terry became aware he was crossing land on which he had fought as a United States soldier during the Mexican War. In Monterrey, two travelers caught up with, and joined, the party, former slaves Terry had taken to California with him, and there freed. Their respect and friendship for Terry, established in California, continued, and they served with him throughout the war.[27]

Terry arrived at Houston on April 15, 1863, but stopped only briefly before moving to Vicksburg, Mississippi, to help defend that city from the Federal onslaught. After Vicksburg fell, Terry traveled to Richmond to offer his services to the War Department, where Terry received a commission to raise a regiment in Texas; he set about at once to perform that task.[28] As his unit passed through Tennessee, the Rangers fought in the Battle of Chickamauga, after which Terry, although slightly wounded, continued on to Texas.

Terry's career as a Confederate officer, after he reached Texas, had two dimensions; one was his normal service in military action, and the other was his involvement with proposals for the reconquest of Arizona and the invasion of Southern California.[29] Widespread as organisations of Southern sympathisers were, when they found themselves face-to-face with a continued military occupation of all towns and strategic points in California, they hesitated to act. Those in southern California continued to hope that something would happen which would give them the opportunity to strike a blow for the Confederacy; an emissary was sent to Richmond from some Californians, who wanted to fight for the Confederate cause, to solicit aid from Jefferson Davis. The emissary was Judge Langford W. Hastings of Los Angeles.[30]

Hastings arrived at Shreveport, Louisiana, on September 18, 1863, having traveled by way of Guymas, Mexico, and El Paso, Texas. At Shreveport, he interviewed General E. Kirby Smith, the Commander of the Confederate Trans-Mississippi District. Smith was not satisfied that Hastings should be trusted with so important a matter, and advised him to proceed to Richmond and make his proposal to the Confederate Government.[31] General Smith had received a letter from the Confederate War Department, signed by James A. Seddon, Secretary of War, dated October 16, 1863 which explained Judge Hastings of California desired authority to organise an expedition to Arizona, and recommended that, should the enterprise be accepted, some capable and trustworthy officer should take command; he expressed doubt as to the ability of Hastings to accomplish so important a task. Some reservations were expressed concerning the funds called for in the proposal.[32]

Hastings, having arrived at Richmond with letters of introduction and recommendation in December, 1863, made a proposal personally to President Davis; the letter of introduction and a cover letter for his plan, dated December 16, 1863, were signed by him. The cover letter requested a commission from Davis for Hastings to begin his plan.[33] The letter of recommendation, dated December 18, 1863, was designated a "memorial," but could be considered a testimonial; it strongly endorsed Hastings and concurred in the "necessity and feasibility" of the Hastings plan. The letter stated "Judge Hastings has resided in California upwards of twenty years, and has been a prominent and influential citizen of that state, holding various important positions of public trust." The "memorial" was signed by M. H. MacWillie, Delegate to the Confederate Congress for Arizona Territory; Jno. A. Wilcox; F. B. Sexton; M. D. Graham; W. B. Wright; and

W. S. Oldham. It is not known if those signing with MacWillie were Californians; the Hastings Plan was enclosed, and included two alternative proposals.[34]

In brief, the Hastings Plan called for him to be authorised to organise fake mining companies which would recruit those Californians who were willing to fight for the Southern cause; the expenses of the recruits would be guaranteed by the Confederate Government; the potential army would be drawn from southern California, and from a Confederate secret society, The Knights of the Golden Circle; the men were to leave and cross the desert in small companies to avoid detection, and rendevous near the Colorado River. When the army had been formed, they were to march to Fort Yuma, California, and capture it, whereupon Confederate prisoners, namely, those who had been caught in the attempt to escape from California, would be released, and three steamers which plied the Colorado River between Yuma and the Gulf of California were to be seized.

Another group, meanwhile, also posing as miners, would sail as passengers from San Pedro, California, to Guymas, Mexico, thence, carrying proper passports, to march overland through Mexico, and rendezvous in Mexico near Yuma. The two forces would combine, attack Fort Buchanan, and then move overland to attain one of two alternatives, either:

"To hold permanent possession of the (Arizona) Territory, keep the thoroughfare open, and maintain an unbroken intercourse between the Confederate States and California;"

or, otherwise:

"Leaving small garrisons at proper intervals throughout the territory; merely to hold possession there of in the name of the Confederacy."

To which Hastings adds:

"And, by changing my mode of operation, places of departure, and line of march, I will th:row an additional force into Texas from California at least every six months during this unholy war."

For the first proposition, Hastings states, "I will raise, in California, from 1,000 to 5,000 of superior troops;" for proposition two, says he, "I will raise in California 3,000 to 10,000 of superior troops."[35]

A following letter, dated December 29, 1863, from Hastings to President Davis, requested that letters of marque and reprisal were desired for three distinct but unidentified associations to be used as an movement auxiliary to his plan of reconquest. He explained that, if the auxiliary movement took place before the reconquest, the Federals would be warned.[36] Since a letter of marque is used as authority to engage in privateering, Hastings must, therefore, have planned the reconquest to include control of Californian ports.

Jefferson Davis referred the plan to Seddon, who rejected the government's supplying funds and troops. Hastings, in a letter to Davis, dated January 11, 1864, wrote he "regrets to learn that the government can not enter upon it for lack of funds;" nevertheless, he submitted another plan to the President, by which he would return to California, through Mexico, and raise 1,500 men "without financial support from the Confederacy." His only request was reimbursement for the expenses of his army, if the operation succeeded.

No record has been found to indicate if Hastings received authorisation from Davis or not; nothing more is to be found of him in the Confederate records captured at Richmond.

There are apparently no further records of him in California, either.[37] Other than tentatively appointing a commander, Colonel William Steele of the Sibley Brigade, who was promoted to a brigadier generalship for the expedition, the War Department did nothing to carry out the Hastings proposal.

By 1865, Hastings bad evidently lost his grip on reality, for, as the Confederacy was dying, he petitioned Richmond to raise an army to go to South America and conquer the Empire of Brazil.[38] In retrospect, the Hastings plan came closer to being implemented than was apparent at the time, for, although Seddon declined to furnish funds or troops to Hastings, he gave him a letter for General Smith which confirmed Hastings had been commissioned a major and was authorised to raise troops in Arizona and California; Hastings had suggested that funds, the principal difficulty, might be raised by exporting cotton to Mexico. The letter also stated the Hastings plan was to be carried out only as far as General Smith considered it practicable; when Seddon questioned Hastings's military experience, and ordered Smith to select proper officers, he clearly had one person in mind, writing, "I should be pleased if a gentleman of the known character and spirit of Judge Terry would undertake its guidance."[39]

It is possible that nothing came of the plan because of the unsuccessful, but disturbing, Federal thrust into western Louisiana towards Texas, in the successful counteraction to which J. Lancaster Brent had participated.

There were several schemes considered by Confederate officials for the attainment of military activity in the Far West;[40] just how closely Judge Terry was involved in the Hastings proposal is not known, During the early part of 1864, there was another plan for action in the west that competed with the Hastings scheme: Henry Beaumont, of the Quartermaster's Office of the Trans-Mississippi Department of the Confederate Army, nominally headed another proposal. He was the brother of the Duncan Beaumont, who had left California with Terry; the two brothers and Terry submitted a plan to General E. Kirby Smith for the reconquest of the Southwest which was similar to the one proposed by Hastings. Using funds from the sale of cotton to Mexico, the men would go into Sonora and draw from the adjoining regions, including California, men who would fight for the Confederacy: Hastings anticipated that he could raise such a force, but Terry and the Beaumonts predicted the recruitment of 1,000 men, much less than the 5,000 envisaged by Hastings.

General Smith and his staff were inclined, at first, to support the Terry-Beaumont proposal, but then decided against it in favour of the Hastings scheme; the reason for this decision was because Hastings had received the commission from the Confederate War Department. By the autumn of 1864, Henry Beaumont was determined to try again; this time he sent bis proposal to Richmond rather than General Smith but, to the desperate Confederate Government of that time, it seemed of little importance whether Arizona, or even California, were part of the Confederate States at all.[41]

A third proposal to invade the West originated with General John R. Baylor, who had won and occupied Arizona Territory early in the war. In December, 1864, he wrote to James Seddon that he had information from Judge Terry and others that a force of 15,000 to 20,000 men would succeed in opening Confederate Territory to the coast:[42] this plan met the fate of the other two.

Although Terry was interested in the conquest of California, he carried on the regular military duties for which he had been commissioned, the raising of a force in Texas, and found that recruitment was slow: his recruitment campaign of late 1864 met with passive resistance. At one time, he took command of a brigade in a temporary capacity.[43] An insight into that activity is recorded in a letter, dated November 29, 1864, from J. A. Roberts at Mesilla to General J. H. Carleton, who was still very interested in Terry. Roberts wrote that in March of 1864, David S. Terry of California returned to Houston from Richmond with a commission to raise a brigade, and also had an order, for General J. B. Magruder, to furnish him with all the men whom he could spare from Texas. Magruder turned over six regiments, amounting to about 5,000 men. Terry had promised Davis if he were able to raise sufficient troops to open the road from El Paso,

Texas, through to California, he would at once have an army of 25,000 to 30,000 men. Roberts also wrote he had learned that Colonel Showalter, Colonel Hunter, Major Kirk, Major Darg, Captain Swoup, and Dr. Madison had been sent to California to assist Terry in his plan; these men had been seen traveling through Mexico to California.[44] As late as April 28, 1865, Terry was still a colonel.

When news of Lee's surrender on April 9, 1865, was received, some Confederate leaders determined to stay and struggle through the reconstruction of their regions; others decided to leave the United States for Mexico. When the flight from the ruined Confederacy began, Terry was one of those who left.

About two weeks before General Smith formally ended hostilities in Texas with his surrender at Galveston on June 2, 1865, Colonel Terry received orders to transfer his regiment. That was the last military order to Terry that is on record; he immigrated to Mexico because he did not wish to live in a conquered country.[45]

Terry's resolution to become a resident of Mexico did not last; after a period of thought, he returned to California, and settled at Stockton. In time, he regained both professional and political prominence, and played an important part in the Second California Constitutional Convention. In 1880, he was a presidential elector for the Democratic ticket; his colleagues on the ticket were elected, but he was defeated. He afterwards became involved in a notorious and bitterly-contested lawsuit over his wife's estate which brought a tragic end to his tempestuous life.

Terry was killed in the railway station at Lathrop, California, by a Deputy United States Marshall named Neagle, the unauthorised bodyguard of United States Justice Stephen J. Field, who had ruled against the Terrys, who, in turn, were infuriated by the decision. Unarmed, Terry struck Field, and was then shot by Neagle.[46] Thus died a soldier of the Texas Republic and the United States, Texas Ranger, former Chief Justice of the California Supreme Court, Confederate Colonel, and California political leader in a brawl at a remote train station; as some in Texas and California would say, "*Que lastimar.*"

NOTES TO CHAPTER V.

1. Buchanan, Russell A. *David S. Terry of California: Duelling Judge.* Huntington Library. San Marino,Cal. 1956. pp. 3-4.
2. Buchanan, p. 5.
3. Buchanan, p. 7.
4. Buchanan, p. 17.

5. O'Mera, James. *Broderick and Gwin*. Bacon & Company, Printers. San Francisco. 1881. pp. 226-227, 229.
6. O'Mera, pp. 228, 234-237.
7. O'Mera, pp. 234, 236.
8. O'Mera, pp. 237-239, 241.
9. O'Mera, pp. 241-242.
10. Q'Mera, pp. 243, 247, 250.
11, O'Mera, pp. 253-254.
12. Buchanan, p.17.
13 Buchanan, p. 128.
14. Buchanan, p. 123.
15. Buchanan, p. 123-125.
16. Dr. McMeans was a former Californian State Treasurer.
17. United States War Department. *The War of the Rebellion: A Compilation of the Official Records of the Union and Confederate Armies*. Series I. Vol. L. Part I. Government Printing Office, Washington. 1897. p. 490.
18. *O. R.*, Series I. Vol. L. Pt. l. pp. 499-500.
19. *O. R.*, Series I. Vol. L. Pt. I. p. 621.
20. *O. R.*, Series I. Vol. L. Pt.1. p. 700,
21. *O. R.*, Series I. Vol. L. Pt. l. pp. 701, 705.
22. Buchanan, pp. 128-129.
23. Buchanan, pp. 122-123.
24. Kerby, Robt. Lee. *The Confederate Invasion of New Mexico & Arizona, 1861-1862*. Westerlore Pr. L. A 1958. p. 119.
25. Buchanan, p. 4.
26. Buchanan, p. 131.
27. Buchanan, pp. 131~132.
28. *O. R.* Series I. VoL XXXIV.Pt. 2. p. 1028. Buchanan, pp. 132-133.
29. Buchanan, p. 133.
30. Cooney, Percival J. "Southern Californian Civil War Days" *Southern California Quarterly*. Vol. 13, N° 1. 1924. p. 6.
31. Kerby, pp. 62-63.
32. *O. R.* Series I. Vol. L. Pt. 2. pp. 648-649.
83. *O. R.* Series I. Vol. L. Pt. 2. pp. 700-701.
34. *O. R.* Series I. Vol. L. Pt. 2. pp. 703-705.
35. *O. R.* Series I. Vol. L. Pt. 2. pp. 704-706.
36. *O. R.* Series I. Vol. L. Pt. 2. p. 710.
37. Cooney, pp. 64-65. *O. R.* Series I. Vol. L. Pt. 2. pp. 721-723.
38. Howell, D. S. "Along the Texas Frontier During the Civil War." *West Texas Historical Association Yearbook*, XIII, 1937. pp. 89-95. Kerby, p. 131.

39. *O. R.* Series IV. Vol. III, p. 76.
40. Buchanan, pp. 133-134.
41. Buchanan. pp. 134-135.
42. Buchanan, p. 135.
43. Buchanan, pp. 135-137.
44. *O. R.* Series I. Vol. L. Pt. 2. p. 1078.
45. Buchanan, pp. 137-138.
46. Guinn, J. M. *History of the State of California and Biographical Record of Coast Counties, California.* The Chapman. Publishing Company. Chicago. 1904. p. 209. Buchanan, p. 3.

CHAPTER VI. THE IRREPRESSIBLE DAN SHOWALTER.

There was a large minority of Californians who would have been glad to see California join the Southern Confederacy, or secede from the Union, and form a separate Pacific Republic; partisan feelings ran deep.

On the few occasions national issues came before the state legislature, supporters of the Union held a majority.[1] During the 12th. Session of the California Assembly, on February 2, 1861, Representative Charles W. Piercy of San Bernardino County introduced a resolution:

Resolved, as the sense of this house, that the troubles existing in the Atlantic States are justly chargeable to the sectional doctrines advocated by the Republican Party.

The resolution was defeated, 28 to 41; a second attempt to pass the resolution was made by Representative Dan Showalter of Mariposa County, which was again defeated, 28 to 43, with both Piercy and Showalter voting to pass the resolution. Representative Conness offered an amendment:

And that the United States forts and arsenals, recently taken at Charleston and elsewhere, have undoubtedly been taken by Black Republicans in disguise.

This amendment was too much for both Piercy and Showalter, who voted, "No." It was defeated, 22 to 37. A new resolution was proposed by Representative Curtis:

Resolved, that we have abiding confidence in the justice and patriotism of the people of the United States, and that the unhappy domestic difficulties, now existing between the North and the South, are not chargeable to the great masses of people of the United States, but are justly chargeable to the abolitionists of the North, and the secession leaders of the South.

The resolution carried, but the individual votes, and margin by which it carried, are not recorded;[2] obviously, the California Assembly were more neutral than partisan in the aggregate of the members.

Dan Showalter, who aided Piercy's attempt to fasten guilt for the nation's trouble on the Republican Party, was a native of Pennsylvania who had been in California since 1862, residing at Coulterville; he was serving his second term as a member of the legislature, and was a miner, as were

Laurence F. Talbott, PhD

most of his constituents in Mariposa County. There is no known picture of Showalter, but he is described by a man named Arthur Woodward as being tall, over six feet in height, with a flaming red beard, and oddly-contrasting black eyes.

On Saturday, May 17, 1861, more than three months later, the Assembly of California had to make a decision on their position, as a governing body, with regard to the War: May 17 was the last day of the 12th Session, preoccupied, of late, with electing a United States Senator; Dan Showalter had been a candidate. He was also a candidate for Speaker of the Assembly, and had made a strong showing, having been diligent in attendance and in the performance of public duties during both of his terms, and was sufficiently popular and influential in the Assembly to have been Speaker pro-tem for a significant part of the current session; he was not, however, Speaker pro-tem on May 17, when the Assembly considered a joint resolution that had been passed and submitted by the Senate, one designed to put California squarely behind the Federal government:

Resolved, by the Senate, the Assembly concurring, that the people of California are devoted to the Constitution and the Union of the United States, and will not fail in fidelity and fealty to that Constitution and Union, now in the hour of trial and peril: that California is ready to maintain the rights and honour of the national government at home and abroad, and at all times to respond to any request that may be made upon her to defend the Republic against foreign or domestic foes.[3]

Under the rules in effect in the Assembly, there could be no debate upon such a resolution, only a vote; this was very awkward for the pro-Southern members of the Assembly, who believed they had been given the choice of voting against the Union, without equivocation, or voting in support of a Republican administration engaged in aggression against the South, which they detested. In spite of the rules, the first member called on to record his vote, Assemblyman Fleming Amyx of Tuolomne County, demanded permission to explain why he would vote against the resolution, which was denied, but the second member to vote, A. W. Blair of Monterey County, demanded permission to explain his vote. The same objections were raised that had prevented Amyx from speaking; nevertheless, nearly every member who opposed the resolution attempted to get in a few words explaining his position. When it came turn for Dan Showalter to stand and cast his vote, he addressed the Speaker of the House.

"Mr. Speaker," he said, as he arose, "I ask leave to explain my vote, and I want to see the gentleman that will rise and object." His usual ally, Piercy, rose, and stated, "I make the objection. Mr. Blair asked leave to explain his vote, and was refused. If it is just to refuse in one instance, it is in another, and I do most emphatically object now to the gentleman from Mariposa explaining his vote." Showalter's retort was, "I have only to say, that no man ever yet heard me object to any gentleman explaining his vote. It is a right which I have always maintained, and I have nothing but contempt for any gentleman who does object." Then he voted. "Emphatically, No!" The resolution passed, 49 to 12, with Piercy leaving the Southern wing and voting, "Aye."[11]

In spite of the previous voting on anti-republican resolutions during the session, the total House vote was at least 71 votes; pro-Southern votes had been 28 against 41, with 43 opposition votes on resolutions putting the blame for the war on the Republican Party. The vote for the pro-union resolution indicates the possibility of about 10 abstentions from the Southern camp by members who could not bring themselves to make what for them, was a very difficult decision.[4]

The Southern sympathisers were frustrated; then, Assemblyman Thomas Laspeyre of San Joaquin County, a strong ally of Showalter throughout the session, took the floor, and spoke, "I thank all the members who voted to allow me to explain my vote — who had courtesy enough to allow members to explain their votes upon an important question like this, when there was no lack of time … and, at the same time, I rise to express my supreme contempt for all those who objected to it."

In this tense atmosphere, the frontier tradition of personal violence, then prevalent in California, was loosed in the chamber; Piercy, irritated by Showalter's obvious reference to himself, rose to a question of privilege, saying, "I regret exceedingly, that the gentleman from Mariposa has seen fit to use the language he has … I would ask him now, as an honourable gentleman, whether he wishes to make any explanation. Showalter would retract nothing he had said and Piercy proceeded to lash at Showalter with words, ending the tirade with reference to his contempt, "I have not language strong enough to express it."

The record shows both Piercy and Showalter were Douglas Democrats, who usually voted alike on both state and national issues; the rift between them was deep, though not political, as some writers suggest, but personal. On May 20, three days later, Piercy made what seemed to be an attempt at reconciliation; his question of privilege before the Assembly asked that, in view of the cordial relations that had always existed between himself and Showalter, were Showalter's words intended as a personal insult? Showalter refused to be conciliatory in any way, and said, "The language was plain."[5]

Laurence F. Talbott, PhD

A gentleman's honour, as perceived by others, was a very delicate matter in the California of 1861; within the next few days, Piercy formally challenged Showalter to a duel, and, under the accepted code of the time, the duel had to be fought. Dueling was against the law in California, but fully supported by the public; duels, were, indeed, fairly common. Friends of Piercy and Showalter met at Sacramento, and arranged the place of the meeting. The choice of weapon was rifles at forty yards. The original place of meeting had to be changed, for, on the morning of the date of the duel, May 25, the Sheriff of Marin County appeared with warrants for the arrest of both Piercy and Showalter. The participants met again the same day at Fairfax Ranch near San Rafael; upon the word of the referee, Colonel Thomas Hays of San Francisco, both men fired, and both missed. Showalter, in a loud voice, ordered, "Load the weapons again." Under the code duello, the challenged party could demand a second shot. On the second firing, Piercy was shot through the mouth, and died within three minutes.

Because the quarrel leading to the tragedy originated during the vote on a resolution of loyalty to the Union, and because Piercy voted for the resolution, and Showalter voted against it, legend immediately caused Piercy to become a martyr to the Union. A comparison was made to the Broderick and Terry duel, where the "anti-slavery" man was killed.

No record has been found that Piercy was anti-slavery; quite to the contrary, Piercy's resolution accusing the Republican Party of responsibility for the national crisis does not indicate deep devotion to the policies of Lincoln's administration. The quarrel was clearly personal, and grew out of Piercy's resentment over Showalter's tactless comments made in anger; Showalter, far from being the aggressor in the duel, was the challenged party, and Piercy, on keeping the quarrel alive, caused his own death.[6]

Showalter was now a marked man in California, and dropped from public view for several months, sharing a fate similar to that of Judge Terry, and having to avoid warrants for his arrest there. He hid at Carson City, Nevada Territory, part of the time keeping himself inconspicuous; whether or not he had been a dedicated partisan of the South, that role was now forced upon him.[7]

By July, 1861, Showalter had traveled to El Monte, California; from there, be approached General Henry H. Sibley of the Confederate States Army, who bad recently captured Albuquerque and Santa Fe, New Mexico Territory, and instructed Showalter to organise a force of cavalry at El Monte. After the cavalry unit had been trained, they were to join Sibley in New Mexico, and become a part of his army. Eighteen Californians were recruited. They began to drill in an open field along the southern edge of the town, near the site of the old Lexington School, and along the Rio Hondo River; by November, 1861, they were ready to begin their journey to New Mexico. It should be noted that New Mexico Territory, in 1861, extended west to the Colorado River, this being the border with California. Each man was well trained, had an excellent mount, a high-powered rifle, two heavy revolvers, and a large knife. Late in November, the troop of California Volunteers, El Monte Battalion, Confederate States Army, moved out. In San Diego County, the Union forces at Camp Wright, Oak Grove Station, had been receiving a steady flow of intelligence, and waited for news of Confederate activity.[8]

The governor of California was called upon to furnish a contingent of volunteers to relieve the regular army from guarding the overland trail, who would eventually attempt to reconquer that part of the southwest Sibley's army bad taken possession of during the summer of 1861. The large minority of Californians who were pro-Confederate, lived mostly, but not entirely, in Southern California, below the proposed State Split Line of 1860; it was widely believed there were pro-Confederate organisations prepared to seize the state at the first opportunity, and feared Sbowalter or Torry might become leaders of those groups. Reading between the lines in the *Official Records*, it is obvious Showalter was kept under surveillarice.[9]

On November 4, 1861, U. S, military authorities bad been alerted by J. J. Warner, of San Diego County, that a party of twenty-five men had assembled at El Monte, to await the arrival of Showalter and others in order to proceed to the Colorado.[10] On the same day, Major Edward E. Eyre, commanding Camp Carleton near San Bernardino, California, was ordered by Colonel James H. Carleton, Commander of the District of Southern California, to "obey no writ of *habeas corpus*" if a person were taken who was deemed to be a disloyal prisoner, and "if Showalter comes to San Bernardino, or where you can get hold of him. If he refuses to swear allegiance, hold him good!" Carleton wrote that he would send Showalter to Alcatraz, and the same applied to Judge Terry. "If any person fires into your camp, hang him."[11] So much for prisoners of war.

On November 5, Carleton wrote Lt. Colonel Joseph R. West, commanding officer of Fort Yuma, California, that he was concerned about the Californian border, informing West that Showalter, with a party of Texans, would attempt to cross the desert, as, doubtless, would Judge Terry. Carleton concluded: "Give me a good account of these two men. For myself, if I were in command at Yuma, and they came with armed men and fought, I would hang them both."[12] J, J. Warner sent another note to Carleton from Los Angeles, on November 11, informing him Showalter had arrived.[13]

Major Rigg wrote from Camp Wright to Carleton, telling him he intended to send a lookout to Oak Grove for Showalter. "Deeply dyed traitor," Rigg called him, for Showalter did not have the excuse of being a Southerner, because he was from Pennsylvania. A large party of Confederates were expected to gather in bis region, the message concluded.[14]

That Showalter was a native of Pennsylvania seemed to trouble supporters of the Union. An editorial in the *Sacramento Daily Union* of May 18, 1861, the day after the Senate and Assembly had passed the resolution supporting the Union, said something on the matter. After remarking that, "the introduction of the Resolution was unlooked for, and its passage a surprise to everybody," the editor remarked about some of those who had opposed that passage: "Three of the members of the Assembly who voted against the Resolution are Pennsylvanians. As state allegiance is a paramount duty of the patriot, according to the doctrine of the secessionists, with what favour can so 'chivalrous' a people regard men who deny both state and nation?" There is obvious anger in both references to Showalter. In the same editorial, it is mentioned that, "in the Assembly, there was a personal altercation between Showalter and Piercy, which resulted harmlessly, however." Six days later, Piercy was dead.

A letter to E. B. Sumner from T. A. Wilson, both of the El Monte Battalion, came into the possession of Major Edwin A. Rigg of Camp Wright at Temecula, which had been given to an E. M. Morgan to deliver, who passed it on to a Mr. Cable, who, in turn, must have read it; Cable gave Rigg the letter that shewed the men passing through Temecula were not miners. Rigg submitted the letter to his superiors on November 27.[15] On that same day, other letters written by Showalter and some of his men, sent from Temecula, were seized by Second Lieutenant G. R. Weilman, who arrested Morgan at the same time. The letters, which left little doubt that the men passing through were Confederate soldiers, were sent by General Wright to the Headquarters of the Department of the Pacific.[16]

On November 30, Major Rigg wrote from Oak Grove to Colonel Carleton, and reported the capture of the El Monte Battalion, referred to in the military communications as the Showalter Party, stating there were eighteen well-armed men who were, at that time, his prisoners at Camp Wright, having been captured at John Wipter's [sic] ranch on a trail leading from Temecula to the San Jose Valley. The capture had occurred at daybreak on the morning of the 29th.[17] The party described consisted of sixteen men, each armed with a rifle and two revolvers. After the initial encounter, the men had parleyed with Rigg, but decided not to resist; the decision to surrender had been made against the will of Showalter and a minority of others. The captured men were:

> T. A. Wilson, Tennessee;
> W. Woods, Missouri;
> Charles Benbrook, Kentucky;
> William Sands, Tennessee;
> T. L. Roberts, South Carolina;
> R. H. Ward, Mississippi;
> T. W. Woods, Virginia;
> J. M. Sampson, Kentucky;
> S. A. Rogers, Tennessee;
> J. Lawrence, Arkansas;
> William Edwards, Arkansas;
> Levi Rogers, Alabama;
> Henry Crowell, Pennsylvania;
> William Turner, Georgia;
> Dan Showalter, Pennsylvania;
> A. King, Tennessee;
> E. R Sumner, North Carolina;
> F. N. Chum, Texas.

Sumner and Chum were advance men who bad been captured near Oak Grove on the 27th.

Once the men knew that they were going to be held indefinitely, they had some regrets. Major Rigg wrote: "They now regret they did not resist. … If they had, they would have given us a hard fight. … There is no doubt that every one of them is a rank secessionist. …"[18]

Statements were taken from each of the Showalter Party by Major Rigg; all stated that they were not on the way to support the Confederacy, and each agreed to take an oath of allegiance to the Union.[19]

The entire Showalter affair was described in a report to Headquarters, Department of the Pacific, San Francisco, dated December 10, 1861, entitled, "November 20-29, 1861 Pursuit and Capture of the Showalter Party at Warner's Ranch in the San Jose Valley, California." The report was written by Brigadier General George Wright, U. S. Army, Commanding, Department of the Pacific, and addressed to Brigadier General L. Thomas, Adjutant-General, U. S. Army, Washington, D.C.

General Wright's report stated, for several weeks, small parties had been forming in the Southern District of California with the purpose of traveling to Texas and joining the Confederate Army. In order to stop the stream of Southern recruits, he had seized all of the ferries and boats on the Colorado River, and said he had "them strongly guarded." Fort Yuma was reinforced with infantry, cavalry, and artillery.

Major Rigg, First California Volunteer Infantry, in command of U. S. Troops near Warner's Ranch, "arrested a man by the name of Showalter, a notorious secessionist, and his party of 17 men." The whole party were to be taken under guard to Fort Yuma to await further instructions.

Orders were given that no person should be permitted to pass beyond Yuma, or cross the Colorado River, without a special permit. "All persons approaching the frontier of the state shall be arrested and held in confinement, unless satisfactory evidence is provided of their fidelity to the Union. … The time has arrived when individual rights must give way. …"

The above was approved in an undated endorsement, signed by George B. McClellan, Major General: "Please inform General Wright that his course is fully approved."[20]

Major Ferguson, commanding officer of Camp Wright, received a warning, dated December 12, from Captain Emil Fritz of Camp Carleton informing him that a party was reported to be organising at The Monte to attack Camp Wright, and release Showalter; the party was reported to consist of 75 men.

On December 13, Colonel Carleton wrote to Lieutenant Colonel Eyre that the Showalter Party had been ordered to be marched to Fort Yuma; Carleton expressed much concern over the possibility that the prisoners might escape, and over the reported attempt at their rescue. Two similar letters were written to Major David Ferguson at Camp Wright[21] and to Major Rigg at Fort Yuma.[22]

The prisoners were held at Fort Yuma for several months. In April, 1862, the commander of Fort Yuma was directed to exact an additional oath of allegiance from each man; shortly thereafter, the department commander ordered the release of the entire group. On his release from confinement, Dan Showalter vanished from the records of the war until February, 1863, when a Union officer, on a mission in Mexico, obtained information that Showalter and several others had passed through Chihuahua two months previously. In December, 1863, the *Carson City Daily Independent* published a letter from Henry Carter, formerly of Jamestown, California, and now First Lieutenant, Twenty-Eighth Alabama Regiment, Confederate States Army; Carter wrote, Alabama Regiment, Confederate States Army; Carter wrote, in the midst of other news, that "Dan Showalter, who killed Piercy in a duel, is now in 'Texas."

The oath which Showalter had been forced to take was designed to prevent a man from joining the Confederacy.²³ Carleton wrote that Californians "would take an oath to get clear and cross to Arizona and Texas."²⁴

Dan Showalter may have had such a purpose in mind when he signed, or he may have believed that an oath exacted under duress was not binding; whatever his rationalisation, be made his way through Mexico to Texas, where he was unknown. He had the good fortune to encounter an acquaintance, Captain George L. Patrick, formerly of Tuolomne, now in the Confederate Army. Showalter enlisted at once in Patrick's company, and, as a soldier of that company, took part in the defence of Galveston. Showalter was also with Patrick in the engagement at the Sabine Pass, when the Confederates captured several Federal ships; Showalter's conduct in these fights brought him to the favourable attention of his superior officers, and caused his promotion to a lieutenant colonelcy. He commanded a cavalry regiment that saw active service in Indian Territory and along the Arkansas River; in January, 1864, bis regiment were transferred from Arkansas to Southern Texas, to counter the threat caused by the Federal capture of Brownsville.

Scattered items in the *Official Records* indicate that Showalter's regiment were almost constantly on the move during the early months of 1864, but the information is fragmentary, and an accurate description of his actions is impossible. In late June under the command of Colonel John S. Ford, he was in combat near Edinburg, Texas; Colonel Ford, in his report, twice mentioned Colonel Showalter's gallant conduct during the battle.

Upon Showalter's arrival at San Antonio from the Arkansas River, he received a message through Mrs. David S. Terry, the wife of Judge Terry, from Miss Anna Forman, daughter of the former Postmaster of Sacramento, and the late commanding officer of the Fourth California Volunteer Infantry. Showalter replied at once, writing Anna on February 8, 1864. On April 3, 1864, a patrol of California Volunteers, near Presidio, Texas, killed Captain Henry Stillman of the Confederate Army, who was a messenger and courier; amongst the papers found in his possession was Dan Showalter's letter, which is included in the *Official Records*, although it was written as a personal communication by a young man to a young lady for whom he had great affection.²⁵

The information therein contained provides an insight into Showalter's feelings and activities. He was utterly convinced the Southern cause was just and proper, and it would inevitably triumph. He wrote to Miss Forman: "I am proud to fight, and, if necessary, die, with the people who

Laurence F. Talbott, PhD

have contended so gallantly for their liberties against such fearful odds. If you could see them as I have, you would say with me ... they are deserving, and can never be conquered." He was convinced the South would be able to continue the war for years, and, rather than yield to the North, the South would "lay waste every field, burn every dwelling, and leave to the invaders no mark of civilization, save the ruins of once-happy homes, the deserted fields, and mangled bodies of the slain."[26]

The self-exiled Californians who had joined the South in state might be brought into the Confederacy, or, at least, provide strong support in recruits. Many of them were convinced a great reservoir of recruits, who might be activated without great difficulty, lay within California, ready to add strength to the Confederate armies, a belief confirmed by the report of a Confederate spy who spent several months in California and Nevada during the summer and autumn of 1864. The spy, Captain H. Kennedy, reported, on his return to the Confederacy, that "many true Southern men willing to enlist" had been found. Even before Kennedy's assignment, the visit of Judge Hastings, discussed earlier, had taken place, and his commission as a major to recruit granted. General E. Kirby Smith had sought to include former Judge, now Colonel, David S. Terry, in the plan; and, as was also discussed earlier, the same sort of planning had been made by Judge Terry and the Beaumont brothers, Henry and Duncan. Colonel John R. Baylor had also reckoned on substantial recruitment from California. The estimates of potential Californian Confederate soldiers that Baylor bad used in his proposal included an estimate from Dan Showalter. Though Jefferson Davis approved of those plans in principle, the Confederacy lacked the resources to attempt the implementation of any of them.[27]

Dan Showalter, however, never lost his hope to bring southern California into the Confederacy; his belief in Confederate sympathy on the Pacific Coast was firm, and he proceeded, independently of Baylor, in an attempt to gain authorization for an invasion of California. On February 14, 1864, he was the first signer, and probably the originator, of a letter addressed to General Smith, that was signed by thirteen others, in which it was proposed that Lieutenant Colonel Showalter be given one hundred men, who would travel through Mexico in detachments of twenty-five each, with the express purpose of visiting a rich gold discovery in Arizona Territory. The group would concentrate at Tucson, and capture the Federal supply depot there; they would then proceed to a designated point where they would be joined by five hundred or more men from California, and march an to destroy Fort Yuma. After the destruction of Fort Yuma, there would be open communication with southern California, and, in California, an army could be raised to sweep the entire territories east, and "establish, beyond cavil, the claim of the Southern Confederacy to the country." The same fate shared by the other schemes to take California was that of the one proposed by Showalter; it was not acted upon for lack of resources.[28]

The complete and final collapse of the Confederate States in April, 1865, ended all hopes of adding the southwest to the Confederacy, or of augmenting the Confederate armies with large numbers of men from California; there was an exodus to Mexico of all Confederates who, for any reason, did not care to submit to the Union. Amongst those who chose to cross into Mexico was Dan Showalter, who traveled in the same party as Judge Terry.

In the March 2, 1866, number of the *Reese River Revelle* of Austin, Nevada, the death of Dan Showalter at Mazatlán was reported, in which it was said he had been shot by a bartender in an hotel at the Presidio of Mazatlán whilst engaged in smashing the furniture of the hotel during a drunken spree. When the bartender interfered, it was alleged that Showalter slapped his face and drew a knife; the bartender drew a pistol and shot him, shattering his right arm. Lockjaw caused his death.[29]

During his life and career, Dan Showalter became the personification of the spirit of opposition to the Union that affected a large faction of the population of California; his violence epitomised the wild spirit of the frontier of his time, and his career ran a close parallel to that of his friend, Judge David S. Terry. Each had killed a man in a duel, and their victims became, in popular view, martyrs to the Union; each had served in the Confederate Army in Texas, and both met with violent deaths. There can be no question Dan Showalter possessed qualities of leadership and personal courage in a high degree; his devotion to the cause of the South was passionate and sincere. Colonel Dan Showalter, C. S. A., from California, deserved a better end than a sordid death in a Mexican barroom.[30]

NOTES TO CHAPTER VI.
1. Clendenen, Clarence. "Dan Showalter-California Secessionist." *California Historical Society Quarterly*. Vol. 40. N°4. December. 1961. p. 309.
2. *Journal of the Assembly of California*. 12th Session. February 2, 1861, Book 35. Department of State, State of California. Sacramento. pp. 194-195.
3. Clendenen, p. 310.
4. Clendenen, p. 311.
5. Clendenen, pp. 311-312.

6. Clendenen, pp. 312-313.
7. Clendenen, p. 314.
8. "El Monte and the Confederacy." *The Landmark, Bulletin of the El Monte Historical Society*. Vol. 1. N° 2. September, 1961. pp. 4-5.
9. Clendenen, p. 154.
10. United States War Department. *The War of the Rebellion: a Compilation of the Official Records of the Union and Confederate Armies*. Series I. Vol L. Pt. 1. p. 698.
11. O. R. Series I. Vol. L. Pt. 1. pp. 700-701.
12. O. R. Series I. Vol. L. Pt. 1. pp. 704-705.
13. O. R. Series I. Vol. L. Pt. l. pp. 717.
14. O. R. Series I. Vol. L. Pt. 1. pp. 728.
15. "Morning News." Editorial. *Sacramento Daily News*. May 18, 1861. p. 1.
16. O. R. Series I. Vol. L. Pt. 1. pp. 33-35.
17. O. R. Series I. Vol. L. Pt. I. pp. 32-33.
18. O. R. SeriesI. Vol. L. Pt. 1. p. 33.
19. O. R. Series 1.Vol.L. Pt. 1. pp. 36-40.
20. O. R. Series I. Vol. L. Pt. 1. pp. 30-32.
21. O. R. Series I. Vol. L. Pt. 1. pp. 759-761.
22. O. R. Series I. Vol. L. Pt. 1. pp. 762-764.
23. Clendenen, pp. 18-319.
24. O. R. Series I. Vol. L. Pt. 1. p. 763.
25. Clendenen, pp. 318-320.
26. O. R. Series I. Vol. L. Pt. 1. pp. 1078-1080.
27. Clendenen, pp. 320-321.
28. Clendenen, pp. 321-322.
29. Clendenen, pp. 322-323.
30. Clendenen, p. 324.

CHAPTER VII. THE RESISTANCE IN RESTIVE CALIFORNIA.

A resistance to Federal authority in California did not blossom with the secession of the first Southern states; even though, politically, California was a part of the Union, geographically she was an isolated community, separated from the central government by thousands of miles of prairie, desert, and mountains unspanned by any railway. This isolation naturally fostered an independent feeling that California had some interests different and separate from those of other parts of the Union.

California possessed a large population of native Californios who had little, if any, attachment to the Union, and a powerful adventurous element that was always ready to shew an interest in revolutionary projects of any kind; the peculiar situation in California during period of the War arose from her position on the frontier, and the character of her population.[1]

A statewide notion that, in its birth, had little connexion with sectional strife, was that of a Pacific Republic; for several years after the beady days of the Bear Flag Revolt, many people looked forward to the time when California would become such an independent republic. The Alcalde of Monterey, Walter Colton, predicted, in 1850, an independent nation would spring up on the Pacific if Congress failed to build a railway to the coast.[2] So, from the very beginning of California's statehood, there had been advocates for a Pacific Republic, who became especially vociferous whenever Californians felt that they had grievance against the United States government; there was a prevailing belief that the Pacific Coast was not receiving fair treatment.[3]

The talk of a Californian republic became louder as war appeared inevitable; many Californians openly resented the indifference of Congress. The two congressmen from California declared, in public statements, printed in newspapers throughout the state, that, if a national crisis came, they would work to establish an independent republic upon the Pacific.

Congressman Burch believed that a such a republic should be made large enough to include more than California; Congressman Scott stated that, if the Union were to be divided, he stood for a separate republic on the Pacific Slope. Other leaders shared those beliefs; a former governor, John B. Weller, said that, if war came, California's people would go neither with the North nor the South, but found a mighty republic on the shores of the Pacific. Governor John G. Downey remained non-committal, but,

Southern California as bordering on the Confederate States.

in 1860, Senator Milton S. Latham spoke in the United States Senate of the probability of the creation of a Pacific Republic. These strong statements for independence appeared not only in the newspapers, but in various public speeches, and in the reports of state officers.[4] On the eve of the War, the question of forming the Pacific Republic was given more serious consideration; a minority, those from the South, had strong views, and dominated the politics of the state between 1850 and 1860. If war broke out between the North and the South, it was understandable these Southerners would favour an independent government for California which would relieve them of the obligation to support a war against their native states.[5]

Though some anti-administration voices advocated that California adopt a position of neutrality, and avoid "any part in the fratricidal war," most took the more understandable position when advocating the establishment of an independent republic: how it would be possible to remain in the Union, whilst maintaining neutrality, would be difficult to explain. The state's newspapers which opposed the Lincoln administration referred to both the North and the South as "confederacies" from the point of view of states' rights, Californians who regarded both the North and the South as confederacies composed of sovereign states employed a form of logic that could well have led to the advocation of a similar confederation in the west.[6]

During the Democratic Convention of 1860, the whole California delegation stood on the side of the Southern wing of the party; when the news of Lincoln's election reached California, many of the most influential men in the state began seriously to discuss the establishment of an independent Pacific Republic. In a letter dated November 22, 1860, Congressman Burch advocated that California, Oregon, New Mexico, Washington, and Utah should call for the nations of the world to recognise the youthful, but vigorous, Republic of the Pacific; his letter was printed in the *San Francisco Herald* on January 3, 1861, with a note that California's Senator Latham had read the letter and endorsed its contents.[7]

The stand taken by the California Legislature in the previously discussed resolution pledging the loyalty of California to the Union, and the occupation of anti-administration and pro-Confederate areas of the state by Federal military forces, shewed the futility of the further advocation of a Pacific Republic; the movement persisted weakly up to the gubernatorial election of September, 1861, but the election of the Republican, Leland Stanford, extinguished, for all practical purposes, its last embers.[8]

The abandonment of the idea of a Pacific Republic did not cause its advocates to abandon their opposition to the war policy of the administration; they maintained a hostile attitude toward the Union cause. At the "Breckenridge" or Southern Democratic State Convention, a platform was adopted that favoured the preservation of the Union upon "constitutional guaranties" which would be acceptable to both sections of the Union, but, if that should be impossible, then the platform favoured the "recognition of the independence of the Confederate States." It declared its opposition to the Federal administration's policy of coercion, and maintained that it was the duty of California to "yield obedience to all constitutional acts of Congress and to all constitutional and legal acts of the Federal executive."

Resolutions followed which condemned Lincoln's appropriation of money and the raising of armies without the authority of Congress as "usurpation of power;" only two delegates voted for a resolution condemning secession, repudiating the Pacific Republic, and pledging California's loyalty to the Union.[9] The vote of September 7, 1861, for gubernatorial candidates gave the combined Republican and Union Democrat candidates 86,980 votes. The Breckenridge, or Southern, candidate, was given 32,751 votes; the votes of the three parties for congressmen were of a similar proportion.[10] Voters opposing a war of coercion against the Southern states were greater in number than those of the southern counties alone. Whilst the strongest Southern sentiment was concentrated in southern California, south of San Luis Obispo, enclaves of Southern resistance were ubiquitous.

The platform of the Breckenridge Party seemed too moderate for some editors of pro-secessionist newspapers; editorials justified secession, condemned coercion, magnified Union defeats, belittled Union victories, and denounced President Lincoln as an idiot and a despot.[11]

There was fierce conflict between the pro-union press and the secessionist press; California had 500 periodicals during the years 1859 to 1868.

Suffering under wartime Union control in California were members of the Democratic Party; Democratic affiliation became a symbol of disloyalty to the Union. Party platforms, speakers, and editors demanded the Southerners be allowed to depart in peace, rather than be coerced into a Union dominated by the North. As prominent Southern Democrats migrated to the Confederacy, Nevada, and Mexico, Northern and Irish moderates gained control of the party; these men kept a low profile except during elections, and allowed the Union press continually to condemn the opposition through statements of the non-coërcionists who dominated Democratic journalism. Democratic papers became targets of pro-Union activists in California; in 1863 and 1864, soldiers mobbed three papers in the interior of the state. A San Francisco mob, angered by President

Lincoln's assassination, destroyed the city's Democratic, Irish, British, and French journals on April 15, 1865, in the most extreme form of Unionist hatred.

Union papers demanded harsh punishment for traitors, and continually prodded civil and military authorities to do more to stifle Southern expression; the commanding generals of the Department of the Pacific remained legally impartial, giving Union journals an impetus for urging popular action.[12]

When Governor Downey, who held office when the War began, made pro-union speeches, be gave little comfort to those who supported the politics of the Lincoln administration, and denounced the use of force by the president when he stated that Lincoln's policy "is understood to mean the invasion of the South by an army having in view the subjugation of Southern states and holding them as conquered provinces." He asserted that it was the purpose of the government to incite "servile insurrection with its train of horrors," and declared that the government were determined on "the obliteration of state lines and confiscation of individual property." Governor Downey claimed, and continued to claim throughout his life, that he was a Union man; as he viewed the idea of the Union, according to his belief, he probably was.[13]

As early as 1861, when he arrived in California, General Edwin V. Sumner was convinced there was some "deep scheming to draw California into the secession movement;" he saw it first from the group advocating the "Republic of the Pacific," expecting them afterwards to induce the Republic to join the Southern Confederacy.[14] Sumner agreed with a petition to the War Department dated August 28, 1861, from a number of San Francisco merchants, who protested Union troops being withdrawn from California for service elsewhere. The residents wrote that California was in need of all of her able-bodied men to fight secessionists at home; the petition stated that a majority of the state officers were openly secessionist, and that they were actively supported by about three eighths of the state's population, especially those that were of Southern birth, all full of hate for the Union, and well organised, and there were 16,000 Knights of the Golden Circle in California.[15]

Although the extent and strength of these secret societies may have been exaggerated, documents and indirect evidence seem to substantiate the existence of such organisations; from time to time, newspapers published so-called exposes of the purposes, oaths, signs, and signals of the Knights. A government detective, Gustav Brown, reported that, in the counties of San Luis Obispo and Los Angeles, the Knights of the Golden

Circle were armed, and intended to commence a guerrilla war in California.[16] The prominent San Franciscan, C. L. Weller, and a former governor, John Bigler, were members of the organisation.[17]

There were two secret organisations responsible for resistance to the Federal government; paralleling the Knights of the Golden Circle were the Knights of the Columbian Star, with an estimated membership of 30,000; in joining the Columbian Star, the oath taken pledged one to resist Federal law, not to vote for or employ an abolitionist, to have firearms ready, and to keep enough ammunition for a "three days' hunt." Through these two organisations, plans were laid to raise forces and aid the Confederate Army when they appeared in California; perhaps the most ambitious move of members of these societies was made at San Francisco, where a plan was discovered by which the Presidio, the Navy Yard, the Mint, the Custom House, and the Arsenal at Benicia were to be captured. The plan was discovered, and the seizure of Federal facilities was checked.[18]

Oregon, Nevada, Arizona, and the northern counties of California were recipients of enthusiastic secessionist propaganda, and the southern counties continued to give strong support to the secession movement; one of the state's first two United States Senators, William M. Gwin, declared California would be found to be with the South.[19] James W. Nesmith, United States Senator from Oregon, wrote to a friend in California on August 25, 1861, regarding the approaching state election in California: "The disunionists for the most part are the most desperate men in the state, and are banding together in secret societies. They want to make California what Missouri is at the moment."[20]

William H. Brewer, in his journal, *Up and Down California in 1860-1864*, departed somewhat from the usual categorisation of those with sympathy for the Confederacy as desperados, and wrote there were many secessionists in California who might be divided into three classes; the first, small but formidable, were desperadoes; the second were a class of Southern descent, whose sympathies were with the South, who do not wish to see civil war, but who would be pleased to see the success of the Confederacy; the third class were those of the Breckenridge Party, who called themselves Union men, but deny the government has any constitutional power to stop the seceding states, holding that, in fact, the United States had always been a confederacy.[21]

There was general concern over the arms possessed by secessionists; possibly the most irritating aspect of the armed resistance was that many of the members had been armed by the state. One such group were the Los Angeles Mounted Rifles who escorted General Johnston to the Confederate Army, and then enlisted therein; another group, the Oroville Home Guard, were strongly resented. During the 1850s, local militia companies were organised at Santa Barbara, San Bernardino, and other localities, supplied with arms by the state of California for local defence. Most of those companies appear to have been inactive when the War began, but reports indicate that at least some of the arms were spirited out of the state by Southern sympathisers, and may have reached the Confederate forces in the Southwest.[22]

Southern sympathisers waged more than negative warfare, and formed guerrilla bands to operate on land and by sea; in 1856, the Declaration of Paris had abolished privateering by the signature of all of the great powers but the United States: when, therefore, President Jefferson Davis announced he would issue letters of marque and reprisal to vessels willing to privateer, the Union were aware of the possibility of great difficulties on the high seas. Responding to a report of mysterious activity on Santa Catalina Island off the coast of Los Angeles, Union officers believed local rumours that miners on Catalina had settled there to support Confederate privateering; the miners and herdsmen were removed to the mainland, and a permanent Union camp was established on Catalina during December, 1863, and January, 1864.[23] Some records seem to deny the occupation of the island by Union forces had any connexion with the control of privateering; it was recorded that the island was occupied as a potential Indian reservation.[24] But Lieutenant Colonel James F. Curtis reported: "A harbour so safe as Catalina, upon a coast almost destitute of them, would be eagerly seized by any maritime enemy, unless occupied by the forces of the United States."[25]

Southern guerrillas, as well as privateers, were interested in capturing Californian shipments of gold; waggon loads of ore or metal coming from the mines were strangely bogged down, or detoured, or vanished completely. Guerrilla bands had a spy system who informed them of the shipments. In spite of the guards who rode with the shipments, a volley from ambush often transferred the bullion to Confederate destinations. Guerrillas fully comprehended the demoralising effect upon an enemy of the disruption of his communication. Without doubt, many guerrillas were plain highwaymen, but most were motivated by patriotism, and had nothing to gain, but everything to loose; this fact will become apparent when the story of Captain Rufus Ingram's Confederate Partisan Rangers is told. Each guerrilla bore the cost of his horse, weapons, ammunition, and, possibly, his surgical fees; his risk was great, and his only reward was the satisfaction of serving a cause which he felt to be worth the sacrifice.[26]

The presence of Federal troops was deemed imperative at certain centres such as Visalia, San Luis Obispo, Santa Barbara, San Bernardino, and Los Angeles; these places gave the Union authorities the greatest concern, but there were many others.[27]

Most of California's emigrants from the South during the mid-1800s were Jacksonian Democrats who brought their traditions and codes of conduct with them; they were embraced by nonhispanic Californios such as Benjamin (Don Benito) Wilson, and hispanic Californios alike, who welcomed them into their families as *comparadas* who esteemed common values, such as skill in using firearms, horsemanship, courtliness to women, oratorical talent, hospitality to all, and, most important, individual honour. As a result, southern California remained solidly Democratic during the Republican ascension during the War, and, supported the Confederacy.

Los Angeles sent strong Southern partisans to the State Legislature at Sacramento, of whom one, James Alexander M. "Jack" Watson, served two sessions during the War, enduring taunts and threats, as a symbol and representative of the people of Southern California who refused to support the North's war effort.[28]

Watson had come to California from Texas in 1850, and practiced law;[29] be was active in the Democratic Party, and, like others, he believed slavery had no place in California. He was induced to remove from Shasta to Los Angeles by his good friend, Joseph Lancaster Brent, with his strong Angelean political base. Through Brent's friendly terms with prominent Californio families, Watson met and married Dolores Dominguez, a daughter of that powerful family;[30] after his dismissal by Abraham Lincoln from his office as Customs Collector of Monterey, Jack, with Dolores and their baby, returned to his law practice at Los Angeles which was ardently Southern at the outbreak of the War. Her leaders were for the government of the Confederate States "first, last, and all the time." Portraits of General Pierre Gustave Toutant Beauregard and the Bear Flag were displayed as a statement of California's independence; groups of men met publicly and privately to explore ways to aid the Confederacy. The loyalty of local militias formed in response to Governor Downey's call for volunteers to preserve order was doubtful, and the Los Angeles Greys and the Los Angeles Mounted Rifles were openly Southern.[31]

Union authorities at Los Angeles were greatly concerned that danger to the Union was not restricted to Southern expatriates, but included the mass of Californios as well; these fears were well founded, for a large proportion of native Californians had joined former Southerners in hostility to the Lincoln administration. Watson counseled with Joseph Lancaster Brent and Dr. John S. Griffin, Albert Sidney Johnston's brother-in-law, in discussions revolving about the best means of providing aid to the South; the possibility of southern California separating herself from the rest of California and joining the Confederacy across the Colorado River was considered, with an increased militia for defence.

It was believed that such a *coup* could be easily made, but that, within a short time, the Union control of the seas would result in the arrival of hostile gunboats and troops, but California had access to neither. Southern Californians who fought on home ground would be ruined; it was Brent's judgment the *coup* would be crushed, and a Confederate Army from Texas, marching across Arizona Territory to join Southern California, would not succeed. The best way to fight for the Confederate States would thus be to return to the South; both Brent and Johnston followed that course of action. Watson and Griffin remained in California to do what they could within the state; Watson began a career as a politician to work for the cause of the South.[32]

James Alexander Watson decided he could serve best in the California State Legislature, and decided to run in the election of September, 1861; he was an ideal candidate to fuse the secessionist vote and that of the Californios, since he was of the South, part of the Dominguez family, and associated with other prominent Californios. The platform of the California Central Democratic Committee condemned the war as an "abolition war, waged for abolition purposes." Abolition was as unpopular with many Union men as well as most Southern men; the Democratic candidates were backed by the pro-secessionist *Los Angeles Star*, which cited their pledges against the continuation of the war and increased taxation.

Watson and Morrison, his running mate, received nearly double the votes of their nearest contenders; the newspapers agreed that those elected were secessionist, and those amongst them who were of northern birth were "Northern men with Southern principles."

The election of September, 1861, was the last to be dominated by the political machine of Joseph Lancaster Brent, who had returned to the South, as others continued to do.[33]

Time after time, Watson voted against resolutions endorsing "the policies of the national administration;" one final vote was 57 to 1. He voted against the ouster of Confederate sympathisers, the impeachment of a judge who bad publicly toasted Jefferson Davis, and a bill defining "treason" as the giving of aid and comfort to the enemy.[34] The legislature adjourned on May 15, 1862, and Watson was welcomed home by his supporters at Los Angeles on May 17; he had stood by his principles in the face of threats and insults, thriving under pressure. The men from the South and their California *comparadas* admired these qualities.[35]

In September, Watson ran for reelection; Los Angeles Democrats resolved to oppose the use of force against the seceded states, endorsed Watson, and, to serve with him in the Assembly, selected the former State Attorney General; E. J. C. Kewen, an outspoken defender of the Southern cause. The *Star* endorsed Watson and Kewen.[36]

Edward Kewen was Mississippi-born, and an acid tongued spokesman of the Southern Democrats of California's southern counties; he had arrived in California in 1849, and was married at Sacramento. The Kewens removed from Sacramento to San Francisco in 1852, and then to Los Angeles in 1857, because, politically, Los Angeles was Southern in sentiment. Los Angeles was more comfortable for Kewen than San Francisco with a predominately northern population.

The outbreak of the War found Kewen pleased with the clear majority of the citizens of Los Angeles holding pronounced Confederate sympathies; every local election between 1861 and 1864 resulted in the election of those who espoused the Southern cause. Kewen was also pleased the Los Angeles County Democratic Convention had selected him to run for the State Assembly with Jack Watson.[37]

The election was closer than the Watson-Morrison election owing to Union soldiers, who were not permanent residents, being given the vote in local elections; even though the newly arrived soldiers from northern California threatened Watson's base, he and Kewen won the election.[38] The *Star* wrote: "Democracy has cause for self congratulation, in fact, notwithstanding all the bullying and illegal voting; their votes outnumbered the combinations formed against them." Kewen bad, on election day, ridden to Ballona, and challenged the vote of every nonresident member of Colonel Foreman's command. The Ballona vote, obviously a violation of the election laws, was voided by the County Board of Canvassers at the protest of Kewen; the Board cited the army's seizure of the ballot boxes, and the illegality of 200 votes by nonresident soldiers, as reason for their action.[39]

Early in October, Kewen's arrest was ordered by Colonel Foreman; Kewen was taken to Drum Barracks at Wilmington by a detachment of soldiers, charged with treason, and sent to the army's detention camp at Fort Alcatraz. Upon his release after posting a $5,000 bond, he was warmly greeted by his supporters of Los Angeles. A correspondent from the *San Francisco Bulletin* wrote: 'We might as well live in the Southern Confederacy as in Southern California."[40]

Edward Kewen took his seat in the California Assembly in 1863, and earned a reputation at Sacramento that made his supporters of Los Angeles proud; he continued to introduce anti-administration resolutions in spite of members of the Union-controlled house shouting him down.[41]

During his second term, Jack Watson continued to oppose pro-union resolutions and legislation; he declined to run for a third term. In 1864, the South was crumbling, and morale in Los Angeles was low; Watson, Griffin, and other pro-Confederates grew discouraged. The *Star* had been sold, and the Southern sympathisers had no organ south of San Francisco. Even without a newspaper, the county's Democrats were able to defeat Lincoln in the 1864 presidential election.[42] To the end of the War, there remained a large number of the residents of Los Angeles who refused to pledge loyalty to the Union and renounce the Confederacy; James Alexander Watson was one of them.[43] In May, 1865, James and Dolores Watson named their baby boy Robert E. Lee Watson. The cause was lost, but not forgotten.[44]

Upon the completion of his second term in the Assembly in 1864, Edward J. C. Kewen returned to Los Angeles, resumed his law practice, but remained active in politics. The end of the war and the defeat of the South apparently had little effect on his political or social views;[45] he was, as was Watson, one Angelean who never surrendered.

The town of El Monte is within Los Angeles County, and was called "The Monte" before and during the War; the majority of The Monte's residents had come from the South, and the majority of these were Texan. In the election of 1860, Breckenridge got 87 votes, Douglass 47 votes, and there were 16 votes for Lincoln; in 1864, El Monte cast 144 votes for McClellan. El Monte was a Southern town in culture and con.viction.[46]

The first important anti-union sentiment apparent at El Monte came after Leland Stanford was elected as the first Republican Governor of California in 1861; El Monte opened an army training camp for Southern sympathisers, and soldiers drilled in an open field not ten miles from Los Angeles.[47]

In March, 1861, Frank Green and Andrew J. King directed the forming of the Monte Mounted Rifles, consisting of seventy men; their old friend, Governor Downey, had failed to issue enough arms for more men. They held several parades that worried Union supporters at Los Angeles. On May 4, 1861, a group of forty men carried the Bear Flag, the state's symbol of secession, through the streets of El Monte, and, later that night, a torch lit parade was held around the home of Jonathan Tibbets, a Republican who had been correctly identified as a Union spy.

In November, 1861, Dan Showalter's men gathered at El Monte, and purchased stores for their journey to the Confederacy; they had arrived as an organised body of cavalry, and took no recruits from El Monte.[48] The Copperheads were active at El Monte throughout the war, and even continued their anti-union activities after the war.[49]

In San Bernardino County, opposition to the Federal government took the form of flying the Bear Flag as a symbol of rebellion. The editor of the *Los Angeles Star*, Henry Hamilton, urged, in the number of January 5, 1861, that the lower counties should secede, and seek admission as a territory of the Confederate States; the correspondent of the *Star* at San Bernardino reported the Democrats there were in accord with those who condemned the war.

Confederate activity in San Bernardino County was a cause of concern to the Union authorities; it was claimed by Republicans that there was an armed troop of horse soldiers drilling at El Monte, ready to attack at any moment. It was alleged that there were many people of San Bernardino who would join the troop at their first move. General Sumner ordered James Henry Carleton to investigate the county.[50]

It was true that, with the beginning of the War, San Bernardino began to see an increase in lawlessness; there was a sharp rise in horse theft, which was often attributed to secessionists who wanted mounts for their trips to join the Confederacy.

The population of San Bernardino was about 1,500 in 1861; of these, approximately two-thirds were considered Mormons. In San Bernardino, "Mormons" was a term used as a catchall, and referred to anyone who had ever been connected with the community, including ex-mormons, jack-mormons, reorganised Mormons, and people who associated with Mormons.[52] Carleton, in civilian dress, left Los Angeles for San Bernardino on July 18, 1861, to begin his investigation; he became convinced the entirety of San Bernardino County was filled with active secessionists. He reported to bis superiors that all of the county, including remote Holcomb and Bear Valleys, was secessionist, and urged that troops occupy the region. A group of citizens of San Bernardino wrote to Major Carleton, and requested him to stop bands of armed men from crossing the Colorado River to link with Colonel John R. Baylor, C. S. A., who occupied that part of New Mexico Territory which had seceded as Arizona Territory, and declared for the Confederacy. Carleton bad previously been notified of efforts at San Bernardino to raise troops for Baylor's army.[53]

Major Carleton's report may have reflected his personal sentiments towards the Latter Day Saints; the major was very anti-mormon, as were most military men following the Mormon War, but Carleton had a particular reason for his dislike, for his feelings were the result of an assignment in 1859, when he was sent to the scene of the Mountain Meadow Massacre in Utah to bury the victims and investigate the circumstances of the horror. He still carried the painful memories of that assignment; with the finding of seditious activity at San Bernardino, he sincerely believed there were few in the town who had any feelings of patriotism.[54]

Abel Stern wrote of troublemakers among the Californios and Mexicans of Los Angeles, and said that he was also worried about the Mormons, "whose hostility to our government is well known, and who, at any time, may join the secessionists in our midst."

The San Bernardino Attorney, Henry M. Willis, wrote to Major Carleton on August 5 that he had gained information, whilst in Holcomb Valley, of secessionist activity in the area, and named those involved and their plans; he reported that a Major Rollins of the secessionist movement had been sent for to address meetings in Bear and Holcomb Valleys.[55]

During the latter part of August, 1861, secessionist activity increased sharply. Although the Democrat, John G. Downey, was defeated by the Republican, Leland Stanford, the *Star* gleefully reported that Jefferson Davis had been cheered and toasted on election day at San Bernardino.[56] At about the same time, Confederate activity increased in the region of Santa Barbara, and Carleton urged General Sumner to place Southern California under martial law; the encounter and capture of Dan Showalter's Confederate Cavalry added to the concern.[57] The community were distressed at the closure of Fort Tejon and Fort Mojave; they felt abandoned. Confederate sympathisers were causing disruptions in the street; Edwin Sherman, editor of the *San Bernardino Weekly Portrait*, wrote the commander of the Pacific Division: "Secession and disunion is boldly advocated in our streets. ... Southern cutthroats damn the Stars and Stripes and endeavour to create disturbances all of the time."[58] On August 25, Major W. Scott Ketchem arrived at San Bernardino with Companies "D" and "G" of the 4th U. S. Infantry, who remained until March, 1862.[59]

Notwithstanding the arrival of the military; the turmoil continued in San Bernardino County;[60] as the secessionists of Los Angeles County fought for their cause through the press and the polls, and San Bernardino County was uncontrolled, Tulare County entered a state of open rebellion; all three counties endured an army of occupation.

In Tulare County, Visalia was a centre of Southern sentiment; Union military authorities in California were kept informed of Confederate activity in the area, and informants advised the establishment of Camp

Babbitt at Visalia and Fort Independence in the Owens Valley.[61]

In the election of 1860, Democrats in Tulare County favoured Breckenridge over Bell, 556 to 350, while the Republicans gave Douglass 149 votes to 115 for Lincoln. Visalia was on the Butterfield Overland Mail route, and, since that route had been abandoned at the outbreak of war, those having relatives in the South attempted to reach their families by courier. When Dan Showalter was captured at Minters Ranch in San Diego County, he had in his possession several of those letters, indicating to the Union army command the intense sympathy for the South that existed in Tulare County.

In September, 1862, Camp Babbitt was established at the northern part of Visalia, and, that same month, a newspaper espousing the Southern cause, the *Equal Rights Expositor*, was established by a skilled, forceful writer, L. P. Hall, printed by Samuel J. Garrison; through the remainder of 1862 and most of 1863, the War of Visalia was fought in the columns of the Republican paper, the *Visalia Delta*, and the *Democratic Equal Rights Expositor*.[62]

The soldiers from Camp Babbitt were not popular at Visalia; they were spurned by the girls of the community, and the *Expositor* insulted them at every publication. Tension was great. Colonel Evans, Commander of Camp Babbitt, complained to his superiors that sympathy with the Confederacy was so open in Tulare County that he felt it necessary to convoy his supply trains with squads of soldiers to prevent them from being raided; it was well known that large contingents of heavily-armed and well-mounted men were moving through the foothills east of Visalia on their way to join the Confederate Army in Texas. One of these groups, said to number seventy-five men, had been reported as "Confederate Cavalry" in Yokohl Valley, east of present-day Exeter.[63]

The continual editorial condemnation of the Lincoln administration by pro-Southern papers including Visalia's *Equal Rights Expositor*, caused Brigadier General Wright, Commander of the Department of the Pacific, to exclude certain papers from the mails, with the charge that they encouraged opposition to the government, incited reprisals, and kept down army enlistment; its editor, Hall, declared he had been expecting the order for some time, as a free press was never tolerated by a power conspiring against the liberties of the people. The order, rather than suppressing Hall's "treasonable" utterances as its originator hoped, made him more vehement than ever.[64]

On October 26, 1862, Senator Baker, Tulare County's foremost secessionist representative at the California Senate, arrived at Visalia from Sacramento, and was immediately arrested, charged with discouraging enlistments and uttering treasonable sentiments; he was remanded to Colonel Evans, who refused to release him on a parole of honour, and placed the senator in Camp Babbitt's guardhouse. The *Delta* was largely responsible for Senator Baker's arrest; it had demanded the Legislature expel Baker, and also find a means of ridding Tulare county of her secessionist officials, these being nearly all of their body.

The editor of the *Expositor* offered the suggestion that General Wright send the editor of the *Delta* a uniform and sword as badges of bis authority; after a very brief trial, Senator Baker was acquitted and released upon the taking of an oath of loyalty. The *Delta* expressed indignation over Baker's release.[65]

Serious trouble began at Visalia in November, 1862, when a group of soldiers entered a saloon, known to be unfriendly to them, and a fight began in which one soldier was killed and another wounded; O'Neal, the proprietor of the saloon, and Frank Slawson, the bartender, were both wounded by the soldiers. Southern advocates formed a forty-man organisation to patrol the streets of Visalia; Colonel Evans threatened to turn the army loose on the patrols, and they were disbanded. [66] On December 1, 1862, an inquest was held; the coroner and most of the jury were Southern, and the only verdict which they reached was that the soldiers had been killed. Evans wrote that the *Expositor* was becoming more abusive of the government and their authority, "until it goes as far as, if not farther than, the vilest sheet published at Richmond," and the colonel added: "These things, being persisted in on the part of the secessionists of this county and vicinity, in my opinion, will inevitably bring about civil war in this state."[67]

A full dress parade on the Camp Babbitt parade ground was interrupted by three drunken secessionists, who charged into the midst of the soldiers with a waggon and two horsemen, whooping for Jefferson Davis; the three men were captured by the soldiers, and imprisoned in the guardhouse. Judge Sayle, a Southern sympathiser, immediately issued a writ of *habeas corpus* ordering the army to bring the arrested men before him; the army refused, in accordance with Lincoln's proclamation of suspension of that writ.[68]

The Army's refusal to comply led to a series of events that included the arrest of Hall for writing an article in favour of raising a posse to arrest Evans; Garrison was arrested next on no particular charge, and placed in the guardhouse with the rest of the Southern advocates. Hall had telegraphed Senator Baker upon his arrest, and Baker called upon General Wright,

The *Fresno Times*, resurrected from the ruins of the *Equal Rights Expositor*.

who ordered the release of all political prisoners upon their taking the oath. Hall continued to express his outrage until early March, 1863; on the night of March 4, Hall's home was the centre of a mob making all possible noise with drums and bugles. Hall came out of the house, and was later found lying in a ditch near his office.[69]

The next day, Hall published an article referring to the soldiers as "California Cossacks;" the night after the paper came out, a well-organised group of soldiers surrounded the office of the newspaper. Sentries were posted at the street entrances to close the building, whilst soldiers systematically wrecked the place, smashing the press, and tossing the type into the street. Sam Garrison, who was at work when the soldiers broke in, was not injured, because he was not the writer of the editorials.[70]

Friends of Hall and Garrison in the north of Mariposa County were outraged over the action of the soldiers, and recruited an armed party of seventy men, who rode to Visalia for the purpose of attacking Camp Babbitt; on arrival at Visalia, they awaited renforcements. Cooler-beaded men from among the Southern faction talked the band out of making the attack, and so avoided a bloody battle.

What remained of the press was moved to Millertown in Fresno Cowity, where Garrison used it to publish the one and only number of the *Fresno Times*, which is illustrated in this book by courtesy of the Fresno Public Library. Hall went to Merced where he was employed by the *Merced Banner,* another secessionist paper; until that paper was destroyed in 1864, and then went to Amador County, where he became political writer for the *Despatch*. Both the owner of the *Despatch* and Hall were arrested for treason, and imprisoned at Fort Alcatraz until the end of the war.[71]

Gun play between soldiers and secessionists continued; in August, 1863, a gunfight took place between James Wells, a local merchant, and two soldiers. A soldier named Charles Stroble was killed; Wells escaped with the aid of friends whilst soldiers searched for him. With money sent to him by his business partner, Wells fled to Mexico. He was eventually tried and acquitted in Merced County.

Feelings ran high. The home of a Unionist was burned, after which soldiers went to the Wells home and burned it; Mrs. Wells could but watch. When Union sympathisers gathered at the *Delta* office, the only place in town which flew the United States flag, to celebrate Union victories, shots were fired and fights broke out: the secessionists dominated the election of 1863.[72]

The secessionist movement did not end with the loss of their newspaper, but continued into 1864, when the commanding officer of Camp

Babbitt wrote to his superior, asking for a company of infantry, explaining that he had heard of a band of thirty-seven men encamped near Kern Lake, that had obtained a quantity of the government's horses; this may have been the Mason and Henry Guerrilla Band. Brawls between soldiers and Confederate sympathisers were an almost daily event.[73]

Lincoln's assassination plunged the whole community into grief, including the secessionists, who felt their beloved South would have been better off had he lived.[74] The soldiers remained at Camp Babbitt until the end of the war, participating in occasional exchanges of gunfire with citizens of the occupied town.

North of Tulare, in the Owens Valley, the settlers and miners in the Inyo-Mono region were divided in their loyalties, as were citizens in other parts of the state; though there were no organised battles, there were frequent skirmishes between individuals.

Early in the war, Southern sympathisers cheered the successes of the C. S. S. *Alabama*, a steam-sailer of about 1,000 tons built to Confederate specifications in England, and launched in 1862, designed to be a sea raider, at which she was spectacularly successful. In 1863, some prospectors of Confederate sympathies found placer gold near Lone Pine, and named their claim "The Alabama" as a tribute to the Southern ship, and a way of needling Northern sympathisers.

Accounts of the Alabama Mine are few; names of the discoverers and records of early production do not exist. The extent of the diggings indicates that the Alabama was a sizable operation during the war; it is possible that the Treasury of the Confederate States received shipments from the mine.

The original enterprise was abandoned in 1870.

Miners of Union sympathy responded to the existence of the Alabama Mine by naming a mine on the slope of a Sierra peak, west of Independence, the Kersarge, which had sunk the *Alabama* off Cberbourg, France, on June 19, 1864; the Kersarge Mine was abandoned after the War.[75]

In Colusa County, the Democratic ticket was chosen in the election of 1861; the Democratic candidate, J. R. McConnell, received 581 votes, Leland Stanford, the Republican, received 348 votes, and John Conless, the party splitting Democratic candidate, received 198 votes. Colusa County was recognised as the banner-waving Democratic county of the state, and Republicans conferred the name of "California's South Carolina" upon her.

Large numbers of Southern sympathisers lived in Colusa County. Will S. Green purchased a half interest in the *Colusa Sun* in 1863; during the War, newspapers in the Sacramento Valley began fighting a small war amongst themselves. The *Colusa Sun* promoted the cause of the Confederacy, sensibly and not unreasonably: the *Sacramento Union*, a strong Republican paper, never failed to mention the *Colusa Sun* each time the latter took the Confederate point of view.

Most Democrats felt that the War was unconstitutional, and believed, as did the South, that it was constitutional for states to leave the Union. During the War, the following quotation from George Washington's Farewell Address is found in the dateline of the *Coluso Sun*: "Every attempt to exercise power beyond these limits of the Constitution should be promptly and firmly opposed." The following quotation from a speech by Daniel Webster appeared on the second page of every number of the *Colusa Sun*: "Cling to the constitution as the shipwrecked mariner clings to the last plank, when night and the tempest close around." The Copperhead Saloon in Colusa was owned by Hanna and Chester; among the drinks advertised were "Constitutional Cocktails and *Habeas Corpus* Juleps."

The military headquarters closest to Colusa were to be found at Camp Bidwell in Butte County; soldiers were never permanently stationed in the county, but did pass through it occasionally. The records shew that Company "F," Second Cavalry, started for Colusa, and, on the trip, arrested a prominent secessionist of Yolo County, and confined him with other prisoners destined to be delivered to the authorities at Camp Union.

The Colusa County Democratic convention of 1863 drew up an anti-war platform, which stated, in part: "War is disunion; that it is subversive to the American principle; that all powers of government are derived from the consent of the governed; that at no time could war have restored the Union, even if it had been prosecuted for no other purpose than to execute the laws; that no free American should desire a union with subjugated states and enslaved people." The *Sun* endorsed General George S. McClellan in the presidential election of 1864.

When President Lincoln was assassinated, the *Colusa Sun* expressed its position thus: "We opposed the policy of Mr. Lincoln while living, but, as our last issue will testify, we approved the magnanimous spirit which offered liberal terms to a vanquished foe."

Perhaps the frustration of the majority of the citizens of Colusa County during the war was best expressed in the *Colusa Sun* of December 26, 1863, when the times were explained in this way: "Our country has been like a ship at sea, without a compass or helmsman, drifting with the midnight hurricane on unseen breakers. The officers threw overboard the constitution, the only chart by which the ship could be successfully navigated."[76]

The City of Stockton, during the War, presents an exceptional example of the ambivalence that raged in parts of the state; Roger D. Riley recently wrote, concerning the diary of Delia Locke, a prominent resident of Stockton, that, although California was a state of divided loyalties, her people found "if Delia Locke's reaction was at all typical of a majority of Californians, the Confederate activity antagonized people generally." Most of the article describes the activity of Californians in providing the Union with support.[77] The Holt Atherton Library at the University of the Pacific, where this diary now reposes, holds, however, other documents which show some citizens of Stockton held very different views.

One of these documents, a letter from Mary Rhodes to her son, Eddie, describes sectional hostilities in California and a probable Californian extension of the War, and indicates strong pro-Southern convictions. Edward A. Rhodes, her son, was a cadet at the Virginia Military Institute, who, in a previous letter, had discussed Virginia's reaction to the Secession Ordinance of South Carolina, displaying his own strong pro-Southern convictions.

Mary Rhodes's letter gives a firsthand description of the excitement caused when "Mr. Beaumont hoisted a 'Bear' flag on a little vessel, belonging solely to himself." The account of that flag raising appears in numerous secondary sources. Mary writes, without equivocation, of her sectional feelings:

The Southern men, few as they are, will never be annexed to a Northern Confederacy — the only hope of peace here is the formation of a Pacific Republic. Northern men will oppose this; it may be that we may have Civil War here. It is indeed most probable if such a war takes place in the East, which God in his mercy forbid, it seems to me that united action on the part of the South is the only thing that will prevent it. To say that I feel no anxiety about you, my dear son, would be untrue-for you are in a position to be called to take your part in the struggle. While I deplore the present state of our country, I feel perfectly assured that the South has the right and justice on her side. If it be the will of God, that this culminates in war, and you may be called to bear a part — you fight for the cause of your father. My father, though a native of New Hampshire, would have been on the side of the South. And, while l deplore the blind folly and wickedness of my countrymen of the North, I should, if I were a man, be found in the ranks of the South.

The above is a quotation from a much longer letter. Members of the Rhodes family had lived in California since 1849, and the Stockton branch of the family had been established in 1852.[78]

Edward Rhodes did join the Confederate Army, and was killed during Pickett's charge at Gettysburg; his death motivated Mary to work for the cause by bringing comfort to the thousands of young Confederate soldiers who had been captured and held by the northern states in prison camps under deplorable conditions. She was aided by Mary Todd Lincoln and Mary Crittenden Robinson in raising funds to buy stores to ease the suffering of Confederate prisoners. When the war ended in the spring of 1865, the memory of the contributions from California remained. Mrs. Robert E. Lee wrote Mary Rhodes from Virginia in 1866, thanking her for her contributions.[79]

The Grover Papers at the same library contain a letter of April 71 1863, from Albert S. Elsemore, of Stockton, to James L. Grover, of Santa Cruz County; Albert wrote:

They are talking a bout [sic] drafting here more — but 1 think if they do, there will be trouble at home — for I will fite [sic} before I will run.

I suppose that you are happy as can be out there-I would like to come out and see you-I should think you might come and see us. Plenty of money, paper money is quite plenty here, but no gold or silver ... The men is coming home every day and they say that they don't want to fite [sic] more.[80]

A plethora of interesting vignettes of California's defiance to Federal rule during the War illustrate the determination, courage, recklessness, political philosophy, and anger of California's secessionists. This large minority of people were held in check within their enclaves throughout the state; they reacted to the events about them, waiting in vain for their army of liberation to cross the Colorado and grasp their waiting hands, and to use their willing presence to further the Southern, or, the constitutional, cause. They waited to unseat a party of usurpers in California who had replaced them in power only because of the disunion of the Democratic Party.

An event which shook the mostly pro-union city of San Francisco was the upheaval over the ideas of one of San Francisco's leading clergymen, William Anderson Scott, the most celebrated Presbyterian preacher on the West Coast,[81] who had been called from New Orleans to become the organiser and pastor of the Calvary Presbyterian Church, built and then used as a place of worship first on January 14, 1855.[82] Scott opposed the compulsory reading of the Bible in public schools, and condemned the vigilante law then practiced in California; during his service as a pastor of San Francisco, he founded two churches, a college, a religious magazine, and a theological seminary.[83]

William Anderson Scott was born in Tennessee in 1813, remained there until 1829, served as a chaplain with the United States Army at age 17, and, at the end of the Black Hawk War, attended the theological seminary at Princeton University, whence he was graduated with his doctorate of theology in 1834. From 1835 to 1842, Dr. Scott held various pastorates in Louisiana, Virginia, Tennessee, and Florida. He remained at his pastorate at New Orleans from 1842 until he was offered the opportunity to go to California and create a new church for a congregation at San Francisco. Although a born and bred Southerner, Scott believed slavery was an evil; like many anti-slavery Southerners, including Robert E. Lee and Thomas J. Jackson, he believed abolition should be accomplished by gradual emancipation: "The South will accomplish this," but "the time has not fully come." He firmly believed that abolition in the South would come about gradually,[84] and practiced what he preached, having given all of his slaves their freedom before departing for California.[85]

The Calvary Presbyterian Church grew and prospered greatly under Dr. Scott's guidance from 1854 until 1861, when the vigilante justice which be so abhorred intruded into his affairs. Scott did not believe the Christian Church should take sides in political matters, and that belief cost him his church and home in the assault by Union zealots. As did other Presbyterian ministers, Scott prayed for presidents and vice presidents from a seven-page manuscript, dated February 10, 1861, entitled, *A Prayer for the Times*. This was evidently a pulpit prayer that included the words, "Sit thou at the right hand of our Governors and the President and the Vice President." When Scott learned of the election of Jefferson Davis as president of the Confederacy, he found a quandary: should he pray for Jefferson Davis as well as for Abraham Lincoln? He decided that he would, but did not call Davis by name, simply changing "President" to "Presidents."[86]

Scott was accused of invoking a divine blessing on the presidents and vice-presidents of both confederacies "as though it was his duty to pray for treason." The single letter "s" at the end of the word president outraged many of Scott's listeners: he was praying for Jefferson Davis! Sunday after Sunday, he repeated the petition to God to be with all national leaders, North and South. The *San Francisco Daily Call*, on May 10, 1861, reflected the growing criticism: "What is worse, to commit treason or to pray for treason?"[87]

A second controversy involved the flying of the flag of the United States from the churches of San Francisco, which had been advocated by some zealous cleric:s. Dr. Scott wrote to his elders on the matter:

Our house of worship is for religious, not secular or civil or political, uses. Built and solemnly dedicated to the worship of Almighty God, it is a place of divine prayer and praise for all nations — sacred to the religious services of the people of God, and of all parties and of all political opinions. No sign or symbol, therefore, should be found attached to it that could offend the feelings of the humblest disciple of the Lord Jesus. His kingdom is not of this world.[88]

Although Scott tried to avoid political issues in his newspaper, *The Expositor*, even as he did in the pulpit, he was not successful; his deep sympathies for the South became mote apparent with time. One of his editorials, which appeared in the number for July, 1861, stated: "We are perfectly amazed at the tone of many of the papers called religious and pacific as the fury with which they have called for blood, confiscation, and extermination!"[89]

The Reverend Dr. Scott found himself at odds with the California Presbytery, and his public statements at the General Assembly of San Francisco's clergy, with their Northern sympathy, earned him their enmity. Some expressions of his convictions were:

Where in the name of God, did they get the authority to call it [the Southern secession] a rebellion?

Jefferson Davis is no usurper; he is as much a president as Abraham Lincoln is. 'There is no such thing as rebellion in the country) but only rightful revolution.

Jefferson Davis is no more a traitor than George Washington was a traitor. If George Washington had been unsuccessful, he would have been hanged. If Jefferson Davis fails, you will hang him, I suppose. What history will call him depends on success or failure.[90]

Scott's speech before the Presbytery on September 18, 1861, was his final expression that brought about the violent events that took place at Calvary Church on the morning of Sunday, September 22. Although the Republican papers for Thursday, Friday, and Saturday, September 19 through 21 inclusive, had whipped up such an emotional fervour for vengeance, that the lives of Dr. Scott and his family were in danger, he preached on Sunday, the 22nd. After his sermon, which, as usual, made no mention of the war or politics, Dr. Scott was mobbed and driven from his church by Union supporters; the mob, estimated at 3,000 souls, formed at the church, and were only prevented from harming the Scott family by quick police action. Scott did have supporters, including a lady with a pistol, but they were overwhelmed; the preacher's son, William, Jr., knocked down an attacker as they made their escape.[91]

The Scotts were forced into exile in France and England; much to his father's sorrow, the eldest son chose to stay with the Union Anny, and later edited The *Official Record of the War of the Rebellicm*.[92] After the war, when passions bad cooled, the Scotts were invited back to San Francisco, and returned on February 6, 1870. Dr. Scott continued his successful preaching and civic service in the city that had once driven him away.[93]

When studying the events and circumstances surrounding some of the prominent Californians who espoused the Southern cause, less-known Californians who worked with them assume historical importance; several of these have been discussed. Others, who left the state, led somewhat notable lives before busting their fortunes to the Confederacy.

Major Robert S. Garnett, who had devised the Great Seal of the State of California during the Californian Constitutional Convention of 1850, became General Robert S. Garnett, C. S. A., and fell at the battle of Carrick's Ford in what later became West Virginia, whilst rallying his men to resist McClellan's army; he was the first general officer killed in the War.[94] B. F. Cheatham, a notable of Stockton, was made a major general in the Confederate service, and fought at the battles of Belmont. Shiloh, Perryville, Murfreesboro, and Chickamauga. The former State Comptroller, Brooks, was a volunteer aide on Cheatham's staff at Chickamauga.

General John Magruder, a former U.S. Army captain on the West Coast, had responsibility for the defences of Yorktown when McClellan attempted the Peninsular Route to Richmond. Congressman Herbert was killed in the Bank's Red River Expedition; many others fought in the East. Thus fought some well-known and some lesser-known citizens of California.[95]

A small but constant stream of Confederate recruits flowed eastward to the battlefields; at first, they traveled mostly by way of Arizona and New Mexico, but, as Union forces obtained control over those territories, recruits had to travel through Mexico, or through Panama, under various pretexts. Some of them, like the Showalter party, were captured. In 1862, a party of emigrants, traveling across Utah to California, met a party of six men from Marysville, going in the opposite direction; they said that they had undertaken that ride of some 3,000 miles to "offer our services to Jeff Davis," as they expressed it. At El Monte, for many years after the war, an elderly citizen recalled the many times his father woke him in the middle of the night, and told him to "get up and get that fellow a horse; he is going to fight the Yankees."

There is no way of knowing just how many Californians succeeded in escaping into the Confederacy, but their number was large; from Los Angeles County alone, more than 250 made their way to the Confederate Army. Enough men from California joined to convince the authorities that larger numbers were merely awaiting their chance.[96]

There were recruiting and training areas for Southern soldiers throughout the state; the Knights of the Golden Circle were very active in Los Angeles and San Bernardino Counties, The main efforts of those societies seemed to be directed at recruiting and helping those who volunteered to get to the Confederacy; it was common for recruits to pose as miners in route to gold diggings on the Colorado River.[97]

To the north, the district attorney of Solano County reported, in 1864, that a former Confederate colonel, James Gibson, who lived at Vacaville, was engaged in drilling and equipping men; it was also reported that a former chaplain of the Confederate Army had been active in purchasing guns and drilling men.[98] J. A Graves, writing of his seventy years as a resident of California, said, "There were many Southern people living at Marysville. I believe that as many men left that section to join the Southern army as left to join the Union army."[99] William Danford. a resident of Oroville, wrote to William Seward, Lincoln's Secretary of State, on December 23, 1861, that there were a company in Oroville called the Home Guard that numbered about 200 men, well armed, and raising funds from unsuspecting people to start south in February or March; Danford wrote it was the intention of the Home Guard eventually to equip 2,500 men.[100]

General Wright's report to Washington of December 10, 1861, speaks for itself: for which the capture of Showalter and the search for Terry were the impetus, but it was really an acknowledgment that enough Californians sought to join Confederate forces, then located only about eighty miles east of California's border, to make a difference of some magnitude in Confederate strength. Californians were leaving the state, as General Wright reported, in small parties, having been recruited, and sometimes given training, before leaving California; some instances of that activity have been recorded in various communities, including those above discussed.[101]

This chapter has described Californians who migrated to the state from various parts of the nation, not exclusively from the South, who took the side of the Confederate States of America during the War, and were willing to fight for their convictions; it is apparent that some, perhaps most, would have been pleased to see California, in whole or in part, join the Confederacy. Even though that possibility seemed more and more

Laurence F. Talbott, PhD

remote as the war progressed, they fought on; many of them probably returned to California after the war, and resumed their lives. Being a Confederate veteran did not hurt the career of Captain Thom, or damage the fortune of General Brent.

A significant number of other Californians who took the side of the South remained within the state to do what they could for their cause; the next chapter will explain the Confederate military thrust that attempted to join with compatriots in California, and open an outlet to the Pacific Ocean for the blockaded South.

NOTES TO CHAPTER VII

1. Ellison, Joseph. *University of California Publications in History*. Vol. XVI. California and the Nation, 1850-1869. University of California Press. Berkeley. 1927. p. 178.
2. Gray1 A. *An History of California From 1542*. D. C. Heath and Company. Boston. 1934. pp. 408-410.
3. Ellison, p .. 178.
4. Gray, p. 410.
5. Ellison, p. 179.
6. Ellison, p. 187.
7. Ellison, p. 181.
8. Ellison, p. 188.
9. Davis, Winfield J. *History of Political Conventions in California, 1849-1892*. Society of California Pioneers. Sacramento.1893. pp. 166-199.
10. Davis, p. 180. Ellison, p. 190.
11. Ellison, p. 191.
12. Chandler, Robert. *The Press and the Civil Liberties in California during the Civil War, 1861-1865*. Ph.D. Diss., Univ. of California, Riverside. 1978. Abstract.
13. Kennedy; Elijah R. *The Contest for California in 1861*. Houghton Mifflin Company. Boston. 1912. pp. 77-78.
14. United States War: Department. *The War of the Rebellion: A Compilation of the Official Records of the Union and Confederate Armies*. Series I. Vol. L. Part 2. Reports, Correspondence, &c. Government Printing Office. Washington;1.1897,pp. 471-472
15. O. R. Series 1. Vol. L. Pt. 1. pp. 589-591.
16. O. R. Series I. Vol. L. Pt. 2. pp. 1018-1019.
17. O. R. Series I. Vol. L. Pt. 2. pp. 938-941.
18. Gray, p. 417.

19. Kennedy, pp. 81-87.
20. Kennedy, pp. 201-203.
21. Brewer, William H. *Up and Down California in 1860-1864: The Journal of William fl. Brewer.* Ed. Francis P. Farquhar. Yale University Press. New Haven. 1930. p. 426
22. Rush, Philip S. *A History of the Californias.* Neyenesch Printers, Inc. San Diego. 1958. p. 130.
23. Walters, Helen B. "Confederates in Southern California." *Southern California Quarterly*. Vol. 35. N° 1. March, 1953. p. 49.
24. O. R. Series L Vol. L. Pt. 1. p. 718.
25. O. R. Series I. Vol. L. Pt. 1. p. 244.
26. Grenier, p. 12.
27. Kennedy, pp. 81-87.
28. Gremer, p. 19.
29. Grenier, p. 17 ..
30. Grenier, p. 20.
31. Grenier, p. 22.
32. Grenier, p. 20.
33. Grenier, p.18.
34. Grenier, p. 25.
35. Grenier, p. 26.
36. Grenier, p. 23.
37. Robinson, John W. "Colonel Edward J. C. Kewen; Los Angeles' Fire-eating Oratar of the Civil War/Era." *Southern California Quarterly*. Vol LX1 N° 2. Summer, 1979. pp. 66.171.
38. Grenier, p. 26. 39. Robinson, p. 173.
40. Grenier, p. 26.
41. Robinson, p. 173.
42. Grenier, p. 33.
43. Grenier, p. 35.
44. Robinson, p. 174.
45. King, William F. "El Monte, an American Town in Southern California, 1851-1866." *Southern California Quarterly*. Vol. LIII. N"4. December, 1971. pp. 317-332.
46. Goldman, William E. *Reminiscing The Monte*. El Monte Historical Society Museum Library. El Monte. n.d. pp. 21.22.
47. King, p. 323.
48. Goldman, p. 22.
49. Goldman, Henry H. "Southern Sympathy in Southern California, 1860-1865." *Journal of The West*. Vol. 4. N° 4. October, 1965. p. 579.

50. Thompson, Richard and Kathy. *Pioneers of the Mojave: The Life and Times of Aaron Lane*. Richard Thompson. San Bernardino. 1996.p.63.
51. Goidman, pp. 20-24.
52. Goidman, p. 579.
53. Thompson, p. 63.
54. Thompson, pp. 64-65.
55. Thompson, p. 69.
56. Thompson, p. 70.
57. Thompson. pp. 69-70.
58. Goidtnan, p. 583.
59. Thompson, p. 68.
60. Thompson, pp. 69-72.
61. "Dr. Samuel George." *Los Tulares, Quarterly Bulletin of the Tulare County Historical Society*. N"102. June, 1974.pp. 1-3.
62. Doctor, Joseph E. "Rebels of Old Visalia." *Los Tulares, Quarterly Bulletin of the Tulare County Historical Society*. N" 48. June, 1961. pp. 2-3.
63. Doctor, pp. 1-3.
64. Berryhill, Richard C. "Tulare County: Hotbed of Secession, 1861-1863." *Tulare County Historical Society Newsletter*. N° 1. December, 1970. p. 9.
65. Berryhill, p. 9.
66. Doctor, p. 1-3.
67. Berryhill., p.17.
68. Berryhill, pp. 17-21.
69. Berryhill, pp. 17-21.
70. Doctor, pp. 18-20.
71. Berryhill, pp. 22-23.
72. Doctor, p. 3.
73. Berryhill, pp. 22-23.
74. Doctor, p. 3.
75. Ewing, Norris. "Blue, Grey, and Gold." *Westways*. Vol. 56. N° 30. January, 1964.
76. Brown, Randy. "Colusa County During the Civil War." *Waggon Wheels*. Colusa County Historical Society. Vol. XXVIl N° 1. February, 1977. pp. 25-29.
77. Riley, Roger D. "California's Military Role in the Civil War." *California Historian*. Vol. 41. N° I. Autumn, 1994. pp. 5-10.
78. Rhodes-Smith Papers, 1838-1842, MS30, Box I, Vol. 1. February 4, 1861. Letter from Mary Rhodes to Edward A. Rhodes. Holt-Atherton Library, Special Collection. University of the Pacific. Stockton.

79. Chandler, Robert J. "The Far West Aids Suffering Confederates." *United Daughters of the Confederacy Magazine*. Vol. Ll, N° 7. July, 1988. pp. 11-20.
80. Grover Collection. MS2G883, April 7, 1868. Letter to James L. Grover from Albert Elsemore. Holt-Atherton Library, Special Collection. University of the Pacific. Stockton.
81. Drury, Clifford Merrill. *William Alexander Scott, "No Ordinary Man."* The Arthur Clark Company. Glendale. 1967. Vol. II. pp. 117, 121-122, 169, 240-242, 250-251, 256.260, 273, 303.
82. Drury, p. il.
83. Drury, p. 117.
84. Drury, pp. 121-122,
85. Drury, p. 240.
86. Drury, p. 241.
87. Drucy, p. 242.
88. Drury, pp. 250-25L
89. Drury, p. 256.
90. Drury, pp. 257-260. 9L Drury, p. 273.
92. Drury, p. 303.
93. Nett, Bertha L. "General Robert S. Garnett, C. S. A., and the Great Seal of the State of California." *United Daughters of the Confederacy Magazine*.
94. Tutbill, Franklin. *The History of California.*. H. H. Bancroft & Company. San Francisco. 1866. pp. 596-599.
95. Clendenen, Clarence C. "A Confederate Spy in California: A Curious Incident of the Civil War." *Southern California Quarterly*. Vol. 45. N° 3. September, 1968. p. 224.
96. J. W. Robinson, pp. 74-76.
97. Gray, p. 417.
98. Graves, J. A. *My Seventy Years in California, 1857-1927*. The Times Mirror Press. Los Angeles. 1928. p. 445.
99. Graves, p. 445.
100. *O. R.* Series I. Vol. L. Pt. 1. p. 827.
101 *O. R.* Series I. Vol. L. Pt. 1. pp. 30-45.

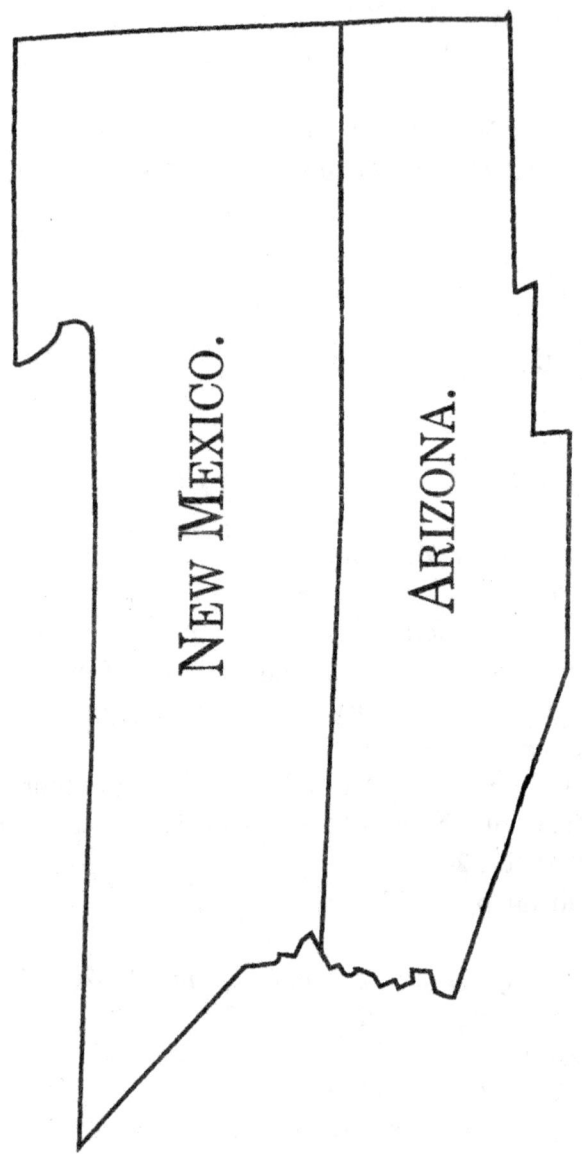

The division of New Mexico Territory in 1861. Confederate Arizona is south of the transverse bisection.

CHAPTER VIII. THE LIBERATING ARMY THAT DID NOT COME.

Although many people of Southern sympathy went east to join the Confederate Army, many more remained in California to help the South win her bid for independence in any way by which they might help; the men from California who, with varying degrees of success, sought to engage in combat as Confederate soldiers, has been discussed, as have those who resisted Federal forces at home, waiting for the Southern Army of Liberation with whom they might rally. That army did make an unsuccessful attempt to invade California and reach the Pacific.

The decisive war for California was fought east of the Colorado River after the Confederate States of America launched her New Mexico campaign, a westward thrust with the objective of securing control of the Southwest from the western border of Texas to the Pacific Ocean.

The Southwest was defined as New Mexico Territory and California; the Territory of New Mexico consisted of the present states of New Mexico, Arizona, and the southern tip of Nevada. Before the secession of the Southern states, the Territory of Arizona had been unofficially established as a protest against the refusal of Congress to establish a separate government for the people of "Arizona;" the present state, together with the part of New Mexico below the Jordana del Muerto Desert, was established as the *de facto* Territory of Arizona in 1860, organised without government sanction, and before South Carolina's secession. L. S. Owing, the self appointed "Governor of Arizona" at that time, claimed jurisdiction below 33 degrees north latitude and 40 minutes west longitude, the people of the region having petitioned almost annually since 1856 to the U. S. Congress for recognition as a separate territory.[1]

Arizona was culturally tied to Texas, and, with the secession of that state, the influential people of Arizona called for New Mexico to follow Texas out of the Union. The population of New Mexico Territory in 1860 was 86,793, but political control was exercised by a small minority of white, moneyed Americans. Simeon Hart, a Texas Commissioner to Arizona, reported that the people of Arizona were prepared "without a dissenting voice to join Texas and South Carolina for the Confederacy;" in March, 1861, a convention of the prominent men of Arizona Territory met, and declared that part of New Mexico Territory below 34 degrees north latitude to be under the jurisdiction of the Confederate Government.[2]

Lieutenant Colonel John R. Baylor's Battalion of the Second Regiment, Texas Mounted Rifles, marched to Mesilla, the capital of the Confederate Territory of Arizona, and occupied the town on July 23-24, 1861; a short time later, Baylor captured Fort Fillmore, and took 400 Federal regulars prisoner without firing a shot. The Union Army was falling apart in New Mexico Territory;[3] because of lack of pay and supplies, they were demoralised and impotent against rising Confederate sympathies and increasing Apache attacks. Because of Southern birth or ancestry, or belief in the Southern cause, many U. S. officers in New Mexico abandoned their posts to join the Confederate Army; even the Department's commander, Colonel William W. Loring, went to the South after an attempt to turn his entire command over to Confederate forces was thwarted and failed.[4] The general collapse of Union military authority in the entire southern half of New Mexico Territory put it under the control of Baylor; reconquest of the area by Union forces seemed impossible, for the Federals had only 2,466 men to hold what remained, and were isolated in a desert without adequate funds, provisions, mounts, uniforms, guns, ammunition, and officers.[5]

Californian secessionists, meanwhile, had been organised in many of the state's counties, especially in the southern ones; in making preparations to receive the Confederate Army of Liberation, they called for California's secession, being greatly encouraged in the summer of 1861, when the 68 voters of Tucson, Arizona, passed an Ordinance of Secession, and delegated a commissioner to the Confederate Congress, which act established a common border between California and the Confederacy.[6] Secessionists in California became progressively more brazen in anticipation of the day when the Stars and Bars would fly over the Pacific Coast. General Sumner wrote to Headquarters, United States Army, at Washington, D. C., that, if Californian secessionists "should ever get an organised force into this state, as a rallying point for all the secession element, it would inevitably inaugurate a civil war here immediately."[7]

General Sumner quickly deployed expeditionary forces from Sacramento with orders to disband companies of Confederates drilling in the southern counties and camps; by September, 1861, Sumner had reduced the state to his control, and blocked easy emigration to the Confederacy; many Californians, however, continued to strive for a Confederate victory. It remained necessary for Union forces, even after the autumn of 1861, to suppress sporadic assaults by Californian Confederates.[8]

On August 1, 1861, Colonel Baylor issued a signed proclamation declaring portions of New Mexico below 34 degrees north to be a Confederate territory with her capital at Mesilla; a quasi-civil judiciary of men having been established with executive authority retained by self-appointed Governor Baylor and the army he commanded, ultimate authority for the imposition of civil government on Arizona was reserved to the Confederate Congress. Baylor began to understand that his invasion of New Mexico, originally a tactical operation undertaken in the defence of Texas, had strategic implications that might make Arizona the key to Confederate possession of the entire Southwest as far as the Pacific Coast;[9] he had received reports of great political unrest in southern California. "California is on the eve of revolution," he wrote in a letter to S. B. Davis on November 2, 1861.[10]

On May 13, 1861, the commanding officer of Fort Union, New Mexico Territory, Major Henry Hopkins Sibley, resigned his commission, and offered his services to the South, under whose flag he became a lieutenant colonel of infantry.[11] Unknown to Baylor, Sibley left Texas, where he had accepted his new commission, and traveled to Richmond to present to President Davis the thoughts that he had for a full invasion of New Mexico, for Sibley had a dream of a Confederacy extending from sea to sea, between 26 and 36 degrees north latitude; he conferred with President Davis a number of times during July, 1861, and was able to persuade the President to grant him an independent command for a campaign of the Southwest.

The Southwest offered the Confederacy a gigantic recruiting ground: from her population of 86,000, New Mexico alone could field a small army: Confederate supporters in California sent word that, if an army of Texans, 3,000 strong, were to be sent to Tucson, Arizona, they would find there 10,000 Californians, with all kinds of provisions, waiting to aid them.[12]

Another important offering of the Southwest was her abundance of recently discovered mineral wealth, including rich deposits of gold, which Lincoln considered essential to the successful prosecution of the war. During the summer of 1861, it was commonly believed by both North and South that, if the rich mining regions of Arizona, Nevada, and California fell into Confederate control the disastrous inflation of the Confederate monetary position would be diminished, or even eliminated altogether, so that the respective value of Union and Confederate paper currency might have been reversed; some officials of the Confederate government, including Governor Baylor, considered the mineral wealth of Arizona to be the true value of the territory.[13]

California would give the Confederacy a Pacific coastline more than 1,200 miles long, and thus, to Northerners and Southerners alike, it was apparent this would enable the Northern blockade of Southern ports to be broken, and oceans would swarm with Confederate raiders from the ports of San Diego and San Francisco;[14] in addition, the conquest of California by the Confederacy would afford a moral victory the North could not reverse. The conquest alone, in all probability, would have been a positive factor in the recognition of the Confederacy by the European powers.

Regardless of General George Wright's precautions and temporary success in suppressing the overt activity of the secessionists in California, the state's Southern-supporting population were ready to fight a guerrilla war in conjunction with an invading Confederate army; although the success of such an operation was uncertain, the probability was that Fortune would favour the Confederacy, since caught between Californian guerrillas on one side, and Texas regulars and Arizona volunteers on the other, and outnumbered by each, Wright would probably be unable to hold the state; as for the Union forces between California and the invading army, poor supplies and low morale suggested they would be unable to stop a fresh Southern arrpy.[15]

Baylor augmented the size of his battalion by three companies of Texans and additional Arizonan volunteers, so that his command numbered 922 men; he had small tactical success, but, by November, 1861, had become well aware that he was in a precarious position from the pressure of Union forces, and civilian unrest by pro-union Mexicans. That same month, a company of Californian Confederate volunteers slipped into Arizona and joined Baylor's army, reporting that the Union had strengthened Fort Yuma, and sent an army east to fight Confederate forces. Baylor was unaware of Brigadier General Henry H. Sibley's approach to reinforce him; Sibley had mustered the first company of his brigade on August 27, 1861, and by November 15, thirty full companies had been enrolled. It was militarily prestigious to join the Sibley California Brigade, and so recruitment was easy.[16]

Baylor remained governor of Arizona, but Sibley was supreme military commander for the Confederacy in New Mexico and Arizona, whose watchword became, "On to San Francisco!" On January 11, 1862, Sibley moved his brigade to Mesilla, and joined Baylor's battalion; from there, his 3,700 men embarked on one of the most ambitious campaigns of the war, completely isolated from the nation they hoped to double in size.[17]

On February 21l 1862, a battle between 3,810 Union troops and Sibley's brigade commenced at Valverde, the first full battle between Union

BATTLE OF MESILLA!
ARIZONA IS FREE AT LAST!!

Fort Fillmore in the hands of the Texas Forces.

$500,000 worth of property taken!

Eleven Companies of U. S. Regulars taken prisoners by four Companies of Texas Volunteers without the loss of a man on the Confederate side!!

Lieut. Col. Baylor, Commanding the Confederate forces at Fort Bliss, Texas, left there on the 24th instant, with the forces under his command, for the Mesilla Valley, with the design of protecting the citizens of Arizona, and relieving them of the oppression and presence of a large force of United States troops, and to prevent the further concentration of troops at this point.

The force under his command was some 300 men, as follows: Capt. Stafford's Company of Mounted Rifles, 85 men; Capt. Hardeman's Company of Mounted Rifles, 90 men; Lt. Bennett, with a detachment of Capt. Teele's Artillery, 88 men; (they did not bring their cannon, but were mounted); Capt. Coopwood's Spy company, 40 men; added to these were a number of the citizens of Mesilla and El Paso; in all, about 300 men.

On the night of the 24th a position had been taken by the Confederate troops, within six hundred yards of Fort Fillmore, and pickets were placed out and every precaution taken to storm the Fort by surprise the next morning at day-break. The plan would have been a complete success, but for the desertion of a picket who went into the Fort and gave the alarm. The fort was alive in a few minutes, and it was evident the surprise was a failure.

The Confederate force then moved across the river, and at daylight took the town of Santo Tomas. Two companies of U. S. troops had been stationed there but the birds had flown, evidently in great haste.— Clothing, provisions, ammunition and supplies were left behind in considerable quantities. Eight prisoners were taken, disarmed and then discharged, after being sworn not to fight against the Confederacy, Col. Baylor telling them that he had rather fight them than feed them.

About ten o'clock the Confederate forces entered Mesilla, and were received with every manifestation of joy by the citizens. Vivas and hurras rang them welcome from every point. Preparations were immediately made to receive an attack from the U. S. troops; and the citizens offered all the forage and supplies that they had at their command.

First page of the news of the war as related by the *Mesilla Times* in 1861.

Fort Fillmore, and pickets were placed out and every precaution taken to storm the Fort by surprise the next morning at daybreak. The plan would have been a complete success but for the desertion of a picket who went into the Fort and gave the alarm. The fort was alive in a few minutes, and it was evident the surprise was a failure.

The Confederate force then moved across the river, and at daylight took the town of Santo Tomas. Two Companies of U. S. troops had been stationed there but the birds had flown, evidently in great haste. Clothing, provisions, ammunition and supplies were left behind in considerable quantities. Eight prisoners were taken, disarmed and then discharged, after being sworn not to fight against the Confederacy. Col. Baylor telling them that he had rather fight them than feed them.

About ten o'clock the Confederate forces entered Mesilla, and were received with every manifestation of joy by the citizens. Vivas and hoorras rung there welcome from every point. Preparations were immediately made to receive an attack from the U. S. troops and the citizens offered all the forage and supplies that they had at their command.

BATTLE OF MESILLA.

The United States troops were reported crossing the river about noon of the 25th. About 3 o'clock the clouds of dust indicated the enemy were advancing for an attack toward the Southern part of the city. The whole force was moved to that point and every preparation made to give them the warmest of receptions. Several of the principal streets of Mesilla converge at the Southern end of the town, the houses forming an angle and are quite scattered, old corrals and the brazilmilly of the corn fields, make the position a very advantageous one for defence. The companies were stationed on the tops of the adobe houses and behind the corrals. Capt. Coopwood's company was mounted. The citizens posted themselves on the tops of the houses on the principal streets prepared to render their assistance.

The enemy advanced to within 500 yards of our position and halted and formed in line of battle with two howitzers in the centre and the infantry, and on the wings cavalry, the whole force appearing to be about 500 men. A flag of truce was then sent to our position with the modest demand to surrender the town unconditionally, the reply was "that if they wished the town to come and take it." They unmasked their guns, and commenced firing bombs and grape into a town crowded with women and children, without having in accordance with an invariable rule of civilized warfare given notice to remove the women and children to a place of safety. Several shells were thrown in different parts of the town, fortunately, without doing any injury to a single individual. Two companies were ordered to take their position on the top of the houses on the main Plaza. The first shell thrown struck on the top of a building on which was stationed a portion of Captain Teel's company and exploded.

After firing a couple of rounds of grape at the more advanced position of our force, the cavalry of the enemy made a charge and had advanced to within three hundred yards of a corral behind which Capt. Hardeman's company were stationed. From 40 to 50 shots were fired by this company, killing four and wounding four of the enemy, throwing them into confusion and finally into retreat, their officers vainly trying to rally them. The order was given to charge four times to no purpose and they retired in confusion carrying with them the dead and wounded.

Capt. Coopwood's company had been continually employed in deploying among the houses and corrals, first appearing mounted and then on foot, and appearing in many different directions. This and other movements, and the appearance of men both far and near, at many different points, succeded in greatly deceiving the enemy as to our real force. They were disheartened by their ill success in the charge, and as night was falling they drew off their whole force in good order, in the direction of Fort Fillmore.

Lieut. Col. Baylor, Maj. Waller, and other officers, were in the most advanced and dangerous positions. Maj. Waller's and Capt. Coopwood's horses were struck by pieces of shell. To Capt. Hardeman's men too much praise can not be given. They were in a very trying position. Grape and canister were fired directly at them. To the most of them the whistling of the shot was a new and fearful sound. If the contest had been a hand to hand fight, which they confidently expected, they would have had to have the hardest part of the fight. They manifested the coolness of veterans. Their marksmanship was excellent, and they in every way acted with most extraordinary bravery.

First page of the news of the war as related by the *Mesilla Times* in 1861.

and Confederate forces in New Mexico; Sibley won a decisive victory, inflicting 306 casualties, and sustaining only 185 casualties. The Confederate army had previously won their strategic and tactical skirmishes without a loss, and now, at Valverde, had won the first large battle.

Sibley lost the confidence of many of his men during the battle because he took ill on the eve of the it, and left the field to a subordinate; it was rumoured his illness was, in reality, drunkenness, or, perhaps, worse yet, cowardice,[18] it having been said amongst the soldiers before the battle that the commanding general "was an old army officer whose love for liquor exceeded that for home, country, or God; this attitude grew after the battle of Valverde proved that Sibley's taste for whiskey was a symptom of personal cowardice.[19]

After winning the battle of Valverde, the confident Confederate Army moved north from Arizona Territory to Glorietta Pass, a principal artery between Santa Fé, New Mexico, and the roads east and north; before the main forces collided at the pass, a battle was fought at Apache Canyon on March 26, 1862, between 418 First Colorado Volunteers, commanded by Major John Chivington, and about 500 Texas Troops and Arizona Volunteers. The Colorado Volunteers had come south to join Union forces from California in their march to New Mexico Territory.[20]

At Glorietta Pass, on March 28, 1862, the main bodies of the two armies clashed with inconclusive results, and many Union soldiers became demoralised by the belief it was another battle lost; whilst the full engagement raged, however, Chivington, with seven Colorado companies, swung around the Confederate army and found their waggon train of stores.[21] The Confederate commander had pulled the soldiers normally assigned to guard the vital supplies, and sent them to the front, leaving only about 200 men to protect the 80 waggons, which were heavily laden with ammunition, clothing, food, medical supplies, and forage for the animals, all necessary for a small army on the march.[22] The outnumbered guards were killed, captured, or put to flight, and the stores were burnt. Next, the Union soldiers bayonetted the 500 to 600 horses and mules which were corralled near the waggons, putting the dismounted Confederate cavalrymen, fighting at the front, on foot without food, clothing, or ammunition: Chivington's coup was the turning point in the campaign for New Mexico.[23]

The Confederate Army were left without any stores whatsoever; Sibley's Brigade, demoralised for lack of food, tents, adequate ammunition, hospital stores, or mounts, streamed back to Santa Fé utterly without order, having left their dead and wounded where they had fallen, and stranded one thousand miles from their base at San Antonio, with Union forces approaching, and Apache and Navajo Indians on their flanks.

The Southwest campaign, from then on, was a series of skirmishes and retreats. After their victory at Valverde, the Confederate army, confident they would be able to clean up the last vestige of Union power in the territory before the drive to California, had turned northeast towards Texas, not west towards Fort Yuma, California; the battle at Glorietta Pass was the first Confederate loss, but a fatal one.

How close did the army of New Mexico come to California? The fight at Picacho Pass on April 15, 1862, was the only skirmish of the War fought in present-day Arizona, and has been referred to by one of Arizona's historians, Rufus Kay Wyllys, as the "westernmost battle of the Civil War."[24] Picacho Pass is roughly 200 miles east of the Colorado River, but a skirmish took place at Stanwix Station, 80 miles east of Fort Yuma, on April 2-3, 1862, between 272 men of the Union First California Infantry, and 15 to 20 men of an element of the Confederate Arizona Volunteers. That skirmish was probably the westernmost battle in Arizona.[25]

On February 28, 1862, Captain Sherod Hunter, however, seeking to learn more about Union agents who, he had heard, operated in the Tucson area, preparing the way for the advance of a Union brigade from California, ordered elements of his command to ride toward the Colorado River: by mid-April, Confederate dragoons had penetrated less than 50 miles from California,[26] probably as close as the "Southern Army of Liberation" came to joining the Confederate Californians on the state's soil. Actually, Arizona's War annals may be extended west of the skirmish at Stanwix Station and the area of reconnaissance of Hunter's Dragoons, about 50 miles from California, to La Paz on the Colorado River; no battle or skirmish was fought there, but blood was shed in May, 1863, when Union soldiers from Fort Yuma, part of a detachment assigned to the Colorado River steamboat *Cocopah* tied up at La Paz, were ambushed. Two soldiers were killed, and one wounded, by a Confederate guerrilla, William Edwards, a former member of the Confederate California Volunteers under the command of Dan Showalter; Edwards had been imprisoned for several months, first at Camp Wright, and later at Fort Yuma. As his captain had done, he joined the western Confederate army; he died in the desert, traveling from La Paz to Sonora, Mexico.[27]

As Sibley's army left the territory, their morale evaporated; the failure of the expedition, the hurried retreat, the heavy loss of equipment and stores, and the pressure of enemy pursuit, all probably attributable to bad planning and management, were turning the soldiers against Sibley, and undermining discipline. As they struggled across the waterless deserts, through narrow sandy canyons, and up and down steep, thickly timbered mountains, the once-confident Confederate Army of New Mexico, in hopes of becoming the Army of California, almost disintegrated,[28] having suffered severely in numbers from loss by death, wounds, and captures, as well as from the loss of material; accounts vary, but the casualties have been estimated between one-third to one half of the entire force, or a total loss of 1,200 to 1,700 men.[29] The Confederacy's grand dream of expanding to the Pacific was now ended.

One may speculate on what might have happened if the army's supply train had not been destroyed at Glorietta Pass, and if Sibley's troops had been able, with captured Federal stores, to reach California; had the expedition been successful, the conquest of New Mexico might have led to a Confederacy larger than the Union, able to muster two or three more field armies, and possessed of the unblockadeable Pacific Coast, rich in minerals. The Confederacy would then have been able to revive her sagging economy, and been recognised among the sisterhood of nations.[31]

The high cost and the lack of success of the Southwestern Campaign could well account for the lack of enthusiasm exhibited by the Confederate government towards the proposals for reconquest discussed earlier; still, California was a rich prize, with considerable support for the Confederacy within her boundaries. As such, she was a concern at the highest levels of the Union military; as late as January 8, 1865, General U. S. Grant wrote from the Headquarters of the Armies of the United States at City Point, Virginia, to General McDowell, Commanding the Department of the Pacific, warning of a possible invasion from Sonora, Mexico. Grant expressed concern that former the California Senator, William McKendree Gwin, would be able to mount a Confederate invasion of California from Sonora, where Gwin could organise those restive Californians who still wanted to fight for the Confederacy, and mentioned that Gwin, as well as J. Lancaster Brent and Calhoun Benham, who had eluded Union control, was in the service of the Emperor Maximillian's government of Mexico; he stated also that Sonora was not really effectively governed by any authority. The letter was not only to alert McDowell to what Grant perceived as a real danger, but to instruct him in what to do if such an invasion took place, ordering that McDowell, in the event that Gwin did bring an army into California, should attack and pursue the Confederates into Mexico, and seize Sonora; Grant added that his letter was "private," and the instructions had been written "entirely without the knowledge of President Lincoln." [32]

The invasion did not take place, but the seething Southern sentiment remained, no passing fancy, but intense, and frequently burst through the lid of military control that became stronger as the war progressed, even in the face of the failed Southern invasion and other disappointments; lives and fortunes were put at risk until the very end. There were constant attempts by Californian privateers and partisan bands to aid the South at the risk of those lives and fortunes.

NOTES TO CHAPTER VIII.

1. Kerby, Robert Lee. *The Confederate Invasion of New Mexico and Arizona, 1861-1862*. Westernlore Press. Los Angeles. 1958. p. 25.
2. Kerby, pp. 27-28.
3. Kerby, pp. 31-35.
4. Kerby, p. 29.
5. Kerby, pp. 36-37.
6. Kerby, pp. 40-41.
7. United States War Department. *The War of the Rebellion: A Compilation of the Official Records of the Union and Confederate Armies*. Series I. Vol. L. Part 1. Reports, Correspondence, &c. Government Printing Office. Washington. 1897. pp. 610-611.
8. Kerby, p. 41-42.
9. O. R. Series I. Vol. IV. pp. 20-23.
10. O. R. Series I. Vol. IV. p. 143.
11. Kerby, pp. 30-31.
12. Kerby, pp. 44-45.
13. Kerby, p. 48.
14. O. R. Series I. Vol. L. Pt. 1. p. 691.
15. Kerby, pp. 48-50.
16. Kerby, pp. 52-56.
17. Kerby, pp. 60-632.
18. Kerby, pp. 68-75.
19. Kerby, p. 58.
20. Kerby, pp. 141-142.
21. Kerby, p. 102.
22. Colton, Ray C. *The Civil War in the Western Territories*. University of Oklahoma Press. Norman. 1959. pp. 70-71.
23. Kerby, p. 104.
24. Colton, p. 104.
25. Kerby, p. 142.

26. Orton, Richard H. *Record of California Men in the War of the Rebellion, 1861-1867*. California Adjutant General's Office. Sacramento. 1890. pp. 652-657. *O. R.* Series I. Vol. IV. Pt. 2. p. 476. *O. R.* Series I. Vol. L. Pt. 2. pp. 459-461.
27. *O. R.* Series I. Vol. L. Pt. 1. pp. 137, 139, 810. *O. R.* Series I. Vol. XL. p. 537.
28. Josephy, Alvin M., Jr. *The Civil War in the American West*. Alfred A. Knopf. New York.1991. p. 89.
29. Colton, p. 98.
30. Josephy, pp. 89-91.
31. Kerby, pp. 131-134.
32. "Letter Addressed to Major General McDowell by General U. S. Grant." *California Historical Society Quarterly*. Vol. 13. N° 1. 1934. pp. 38-39.

CHAPTER IX. THE PRIVATEERS.

SAN FRANCISCO, well aware of her commercial and strategic importance during the War, was largely pro-union. Attention was directed to the problems of the defence of the Bay, with the Mare Island Navy Yard, and the defence of the coast; the duties of the United States Pacific Squadron, consisting of the defence of the coastline and the performance of customary diplomatic missions, were greatly increased at a time when Federal warships were urgently needed to blockade the Confederate States.[1]

Confederate leaders knew that, by halting the flow of California's gold, they would weaken the Union's credit and purchasing power, and planned to intercept shipments of gold moving through the sea lanes of the Pacific Coast; naval records tell how John T. Pickett, Confederate Agent in Mexico, attempted to outfit privateers for operations in Californian waters. Privateering presented a great threat to the Union which preoccupied the U.S. Pacific Squadron.

John B. Montgomery, Commodore of the Pacific Squadron, sought to provide additional security in the Gulf of California to "guard against possible piratical intrusions" off Cape San Lucas at the tip of Baja California; he believed Confederate privateers were more likely to operate near Cape San Lucas, where there were strong winds. Because coal could be procured only at government depôts or at the docks of the mail steamship company, Montgomery thought any privateering along the Panama Route would carried on in sailing ships; on his knowledge that two bays, Magdalena and St. Bartholomew, were suitable for privateer rendezvous, he placed his squadron along the west coast of Baja California. Throughout the War, Pacific Squadron commanders considered their forces inadequate to protect the commerce of the United States from Confederate privateers, and continually requested new warships; there were reports from both Mexico and Canada that Confederate agents were attempting to procure schooners and outfit them as privateers. A group of San Franciscans had attempted such a transaction at Mazatlan; the *Victoria Chronicle* of Vancouver, B.C., carried an article in its number of February 4, 1863, telling an alleged Confederate commodore had arrived at Victoria. He supposedly held a commission signed by Jefferson Davis, and was authorised to purchase a British vessel as a privateer to sail south and capture a streamer with a cargo of Californian gold; it was later speculated whether the British Columbian activity may have been part of Asbury Harpending's search for a ship.

As previously discussed, Santa Catalina Island, opposite Los Angeles Harbour, was occupied from January 2 to September 15, 1864, by the 4th California Infantry from Drum Barracks at Wilmington; Union authorities believed that civilians on the island were involved in a covert operation to seize the island as a rendezvous for privateers. As late as November, 1864, seven enlisted men of the Confederate Navy were captured attempting to seize the steamer *Salvador* off the coast of Panama; the Confederate sailors were court-martialed rather than held as prisoners of war.[2] By and large, members of the Confederate Navy were treated as pirates by the North: Asbury Harpending's role in the Chapman Affair is a case in point.

Harpending, a Kentuckian, had accumulated a fortune in the mines of California and Mexico; when he met Jefferson Davis, his father was one of the largest landed proprietors of the southwestern section of Kentucky.[3] He ran away from college at the age of 15, and enlisted under General Charles J. Walker, the "Fillibuster," who set out to conquer Nicaragua.[4] After some adventures in Mexico, Harpending returned to San Francisco in the autumn of 1860; before he was twenty, he had more than $250,000 in the bank and a mine in Mexico he claimed was worth a million dollars. The election of Abraham Lincoln to the presidency occurred immediately after his arrival at San Francisco.

It occurred to Harpending, and to others in California, that if California, the isolated state on the Pacific, joined the Confederacy, the city of San Francisco and her impregnable fortifications would be able to halt the outflow of gold; Harpending believed the Union cause depended upon this gold, and he and other Southern sympathisers believed California would be connected through "savage Arizona to Texas." He saw the advantage which the Confederacy would have by the control of the Pacific. An opportunity arose for him to join with a group of conspirators, whom Harpending described as having prominent men of San Francisco in their number; their spokesman was described as "a great man of affairs." Taking an oath of secrecy, Harpending was ready to serve the South in any way that he could; thus, he became one of a society of thirty members, pledged to carry California out of the Union, who addressed their leader as "General." Each member would command a fighting force of about 100 men who had been recruited from the ranks of Mexican War veterans, ex-Indian fighters, and any Southerner eager to join any undertaking which promised adventure, all of whom were devoted to the Southern cause. The organisation planned to paralyse Union resistance by simultaneous attack; the Federal Army were undermanned, and the conspirators intended to take Fort Point, Alcatraz, Mare Island, and the arsenal at Benicia, planning to form the Republic of the Pacific as an act preliminary to her joining the Confederacy, and all was ready by the middle of January, 1861.[5]

The group met with General Albert Sidney Johnston to ask his support; it was assumed he would join them, as Unionists had accused him of being a Southern sympathiser. They had not reckoned with his sense of duty as long as he carried a commission in the United States Army. Johnston's statement, "I have heard foolish talk about an attempt to seize strongholds of the government under my charge. Knowing this, I have prepared for emergencies, and will defend the property of the United States with every resource at my command, and with the last drop of blood in my body." Johnston's loyalty to his uniform, and his knowledge of the plot to seize the city, put a stop to the Society's plan; the group disbanded by a vote of secret ballot.[6]

Asbury Harpending was brokenhearted at the failure of the venture; he and his friends began to consider the idea of intercepting the gold shipments. Since many were sent on ships by the Pacific Mail, these ships might be seized on the high seas. Harpending said he had no desire to participate in piracy, but was ready for the risk involved in capturing Union shipping off the West Coast. He traveled to Richmond, Virginia, by way of Mexico City and Veracruz, to obtain a regular commission from the Confederate Navy. Within the generally accepted rules of war, this commission would allow him to engage as a privateer in the capture of gold-bearing mail steamers.[7]

Shortly after his arrival, Asbury Harpending was able to meet with the Confederate president and present his plans; the president showed great interest, and required several further interviews. He did not come to a swift conclusion, but consulted with Judah Benjamin, the Confederate Attorney General, who scrutinised Harpending's plan with great care, especially the questions regarding piracy. Benjamin gave his opinion to the president that it would be entirely within the scope of international law to equip and sail a vessel out of any port of the United States, provided no overt act against commerce were committed before a foreign port had been reached; letters of marque should be exhibited, and the open purpose of those in command should be declared.[8]

President Davis saw the importance of shutting off the great gold shipments to the East; his stated opinion was that the success of such a venture would be more important than many victories in the field. At the same time, he realised the serious difficulties of outfitting a privateer at any of the Pacific ports without arousing suspicion. Asbury Harpending received a commission as a captain in the Confederate Navy, as well as letters of marque in blank, the names to be filled in after the ship had reached a foreign port; he was also entrusted with a large bundle of mail addressed to prominent Southerners in California.[9]

Harpending, ready to begin his privateering adventure, returned to California in late July, 1862, and found only one of his former comrades, Ridgley Greathouse, remained interested in the venture. Greathouse was connected with some of the well known families of California and the South. The two of them decided to proceed and outfit their Confederate privateer on their own. An unexpected ally joined them almost immediately; he was Alfred Rubery, a young English gentleman, the nephew of John Bright, the English statesman,[10] who had traveled through the South just before the War, where he acquired an admiration for the Southern aristocracy. The three young men worked well together. Harpending's first intention was to outfit the ship in British Columbia; this may have started the rumour about the "Confederate commodore." Another ship in Oregon was considered, but this proved to be too slow.

Whilst the three hopeful privateers became impatient with the delay, a small deep-water vessel came into the port of San Francisco after a record-breaking voyage from New York, named the *Chapman*. Harpending never understood why historians later wrote that it was the "*J. M. Chapman*." The *Chapman* was purchased from her owners, and the operation was set in motion. The privateers proposed to sail the *Chapman* to some islands off the Mexican Coast, outfit her into a fighting craft, and proceed to Manzanillo, where they would present the letters of marque and Harpending's commission as a captain in the Confederate Navy. They would then lie in wait for the first Pacific Mail packet that entered the harbour, and there capture her. They would then equip the captured packet as a privateer, and intercept two more eastbound Pacific Mail steamers before their presence was discovered.

Now that they had their ship, other preparations began. Two 12-pound cannons were purchased, as were shells, shot, and large quantities of other ammunition, together with a large assortment of small arms that included rifles, revolvers, and cutlasses. Everything was crated and marked "machinery." To avoid suspicion, they also laid in a small line of general goods which were saleable at a Mexican port; a reserve of provisions was also put on board.

A crew of twenty Southern able seamen were picked, considered to be "of proven and desperate courage." They did not know one other, and were told only that their mission involved lots of fighting.[11]

Bancroft lists the "conspirators," besides Greathouse:

Alfred Rubery, England;
W. W. Mason, Alabama, nephew of the Confederate Commander in England;
Asbury Harpending, Kentucky;
Alborn T. Crow, late of the Confederate Army;
John E. Kent, Illinois'
William C. Low (Law), New York. Commander who turned state's evidence;
Lorenzo L. Libby, First Officer;
Thomas Reole (Poole);
Joseph W. Smith, alias Snyder, Kentucky;
Alfred Armond, Ottawa, C. W.;
Henry C. Boyd, Delaware;
R. H. Duval, Florida;
William D. Moore;
J. W. McFadden;
William W. Maron;
D. W. Brown;
John Fletcher;
James E. Smith;
George W. Davis;
M. H. Marshall;
Five sailors and cabin boys.

The list shows 21 men rather than 20 as listed in Harpending's memoirs; he does not list W. W. Mason as a leader. Captain Law is listed as "Low" and Thomas "Reole" must have been Thomas Bell Poole, who is known to have participated aboard the *Chapman*.[12]

Finding a navigator proved most difficult, for few Southern men had much practical experience in seamanship. William Law, who claimed a knowledge of Pacific waters and patriotism for the South, was recommended for the position. He seemed untrustworthy to Harpending, and was dismissed at first, but time was passing by, and he was the only applicant; so, he was reluctantly given the office. He had to know the plans of the operation if he were to navigate. One other officer was employed to be the sailing master, Lorenzo L. Libby. Clearance papers were issued by the Port of San Francisco Customs House, perhaps too easily; the *Chapman* was duly certified to sail to Manzanillo with a cargo of machinery and mixed merchandise.[13]

Laurence F. Talbott, PhD

On the night of March 14, 1862, Greathouse and Law were to be aboard the *Chapman*, whilst Harpending and Rubery met with the fighting men. When all was ready, they came aboard the privateer in three groups to find an agitated Greathouse; Law had not kept his appointment. The *Chapman* was cast loose from the wharf, and anchored in the stream; as they could not sail without their navigator, they had to wait. They waited all night, and, as the sun rose, they found themselves looking into the trained guns of the USS *Cyane*; several boatloads of officers and marines were heading for the *Chapman*. Resistance was useless: Harpending, Greathouse, and Rubery proceeded to destroy as many papers as possible before they were taken.[14]

The search party found the naval cargo, and took the fighting men by surprise; William Law had betrayed them. Harpending and his officers took full responsibility, and stated their men were employed only for service in Mexico; none were prosecuted, and, finally, all were discharged. Harpending, Greathouse, Rubery, and Libby were informed they were charged with piracy; the four were first taken to Alcatraz, and then to the Old Broadway Gaol.

Law had made a traitor's bargain with the authorities, and made a small fortune by his treachery; he had disclosed all of the plans, and the men of the *Chapman* had been under observation by agents of the U.S. Navy for days before their capture. Harpending, Rubery, and Libby were imprisoned for six months; Greathouse was released on bail whilst the government prepared the trial.[15]

A San Francisco newspaper, the *American Flag*, demanded the four be tried for the capital offence of piracy; the government's judgment was that such a charge was untenable, and so the final indictment was high treason. Only Law's word provided the government any evidence; the men and arms on the *Chapman* might have been intended for use on a fillibuster expedition against a Central American state. The false Customs House papers and the secret preparations for leaving port could be explained in the same manner; every one had known that the defendants had been Southern sympathisers for some time, and so any Southern literature found on their person would come as no surprise. There was much suspicion, but no proof, until Greathouse made some dire predictions which frightened Libby into confessing everything; he was the only one of the four without influence in California, for he was a Canadian.[16]

The accused were brought to trial on October 2, 1862, in the United States Circuit Court; Law and Libby both testified against their comrades, which established the charge of high treason.[17] The indictment charged the trio with outfitting the schooner for use under "said pretended government called the Confederate States of America, against the United States of America, as afore said, to cruise the high seas and commit hostilities upon citizens, property, and vessels of the United States of America on the pretense of the authority of a letter of marque by one Jefferson Davis, a president of the Confederate States of America aforesaid."[18]

The government proved that Greathouse and Harpending were citizens of the United States, not of the seceded states: one might note this as a juridical recognition of the Confederate States of America. The defendants were found guilty of high treason, and each was sentenced to ten years' imprisonment and a fine of $1,000. United States authorities secretly placed Law and Libby on board of a ship bound for China, and the pair were never heard from again; thus ended the "*Chapman* Affair."

After a brief confinement, Greathouse was released under a General Amnesty Act, and, upon taking an oath of allegiance, Rubery was pardoned by President Lincoln at the request of his union-supporting British uncle, John Bright; Rubery returned to England. Because he held a commission in the Confederate Navy, Harpending was detained; four months after his sentence, Harpending was ordered to be released under the Amnesty Act, and the fine was remitted.[19] Harpending returned to mining for the remainder of the war.[20]

After the *Chapman* Affair had been made public, a new wave of fear gripped San Francisco; the authorities renewed their efforts to improve the defences of the harbour, and serious study was given to the idea of erecting fortifications on Yerba Buena Island and at Rincon Point, in order to protect the inner harbour.[21]

NOTES TO CHAPTER IX

1. Gilbert, Benjamin Franklin. "San Francisco Harbour Defence during the Civil War." *California Historical Society Quarterly*. Vol. 33. N° 3. September, 1954. p. 229.
2. Gilbert, Benjamin Franklin. "Confederate Privateers in California." *The Californians*. Jan./Feb., 1985. pp. 19-23.
3. Camp, William Martin. *San Francisco: Port of Gold*. Doubleday and Company, Inc. Garden City. 1947. p. 122.
4. Harpending, Asbury. *The Great Diamond Hoax and Other Stirring Incidents in the Life of Asbury Harpending*. Ed. James H. Wilkins. The James H. Barry Co. San Francisco. 1913. p. 11.
5. Harpending, pp. 22-31.

6. Harpending, pp. 36-38.
7. Harpending, p. 46.
8. Harpending, p. 48.
9. Harpending, pp. 47-48.
10. Harpending, pp. 65-66.
11. Harpending, pp. 73-75.
12. Harpending, p. 74.
13. Bancroft, Hubert Howe. *The Works of Hubert Howe Bancroft*. Vol. VII. of *History of California*. 1860-1890. The History Company Publishers. San Francisco. 1890. pp. 187-288.
14. Harpending, pp. 75-76.
15. Harpending, pp. 76-78.
16. Harpending, pp. 80-83.
17. Harpending, pp. 83-85.
18. Harpending, p. 86.
19. Camp, p. 144.
20. Harpending, pp. 86-90.
21. Harpending, p. 107.

CHAPTER X. PARTISAN RANGERS.

Before presenting a narrative of guerrilla warfare in California, it may be well to provide a brief discussion, in general terms, of the character and role of partisans who engaged in military action during the War; this is done to preclude, or at least counter, the oft-voiced allegation that those who claimed to be Confederate guerrillas in California were rather, most likely, ordinary outlaws without any motive but plunder.

It should be understood that partisans, whether, called partisan rangers or guerrilla bands, were not, or ever claimed to be, regular troops, but operated in relatively small units, primarily in territory controlled by the enemy, or at least containing a strong enemy presence, usually from a home base, or bases located where they had at least the ideological, if not more tangible, support of a significant portion of the population; when away from the home base, partisans lived off of the enemy and the land which they were raiding.

Bands of partisan rangers fought guerrilla warfare in all theaters of the war; their objectives included crippling enemy movements by cutting telegraph lines, tearing up railway tracks, and burning bridges. When circumstances warranted the deed, they killed the enemy. It is difficult to differentiate between partisan rangers and guerrilla bands, for the terms are commonly used synonymously: by either designation, all were engaged in the same type of warfare. The bands which claimed legitimacy because of recognition by an established government tended to be called "rangers" where such recognition was not granted, partisan bands tended to be known as "guerrillas." Although those of either designation could be recognised units, the more violent acts seem to be attributed to "guerrillas."

Partisans burned structures, killed the enemy, stole horses, robbed banks, made war on civilians, and either paroled or killed enemies taken captive, and behaved very much as did the regular army of General William Tecumseh Sherman on their march through Georgia, but on a smaller scale; guerrilla bands broke up into small units and raided over widely dispersed areas which made them difficult to catch.

Both the North and the South had partisan support; the Northern partisans began operations before the War in Kansas and Missouri, when Jayhawkers fought against United States troops and pro-Southern settlers as Abolitionists or Free Soilers. Their outrages in the late 1850s brought indictments by the courts of the United States; some leaders were taken into custody by the U. S. Army, but, with the beginning of the War, the Northern partisans became "Union Militia" or "Home Guards" and President Lincoln made Senator James Henry Lane, a founder of partisan bands and one of their bloodiest leaders, a Brigadier General. Lane's lieutenant, Charles R. Jennison, was arrested during the war for indiscriminate looting of both Northern and Southern sympathisers, although powerful abolitionists in Kansas and Washington enabled him to retain his rank of colonel of militia, and continue his "non-partisan" depredations.[1]

The South responded in kind with raiders such as William Clark Quantrill, George Todd, William T. "Bloody Bill" Anderson, Cole Younger, and Frank and Jesse James, who raided into Kansas, and attacked Union points in Missouri.[2]

The growing number of Confederate partisans, and the frequency of their devastating raids, caused the Union Major General Henry Halleck, Commander of the Department of the West, to issue General Order Number Two on March 13, 1862, which branded all Confederate guerrillas as outlaws, and required they be executed upon capture;[3] on April 22, 1862, the Confederate Congress passed a bill that authorised the formation of bands of partisan rangers, the purpose of the act being to bring existing bands, fighting in the field, under the control of the command of the regular army, and give them a semblance of legality. The act authorised President Jefferson Davis to commission officers "with authority to form bands of partisan rangers in companies, battalions, or regiments … such partisan rangers, after being regularly received into service, shall be entitled to the same pay, rations, and quarters during their terms of service, and are subject to the same regulations as other soldiers."

A simplified version of the act was published by General Thomas C. Hindman to authorise the practice of guerrilla warfare in Arkansas, which stated, once a band of ten or more men had come together and armed themselves, they might elect their leaders, and begin operations against the enemy without waiting to be mustered in or receive orders; companies of partisan rangers were supposed to report to Confederate authorities at the first opportunity, but most of them never did.[4]

Union military authorities consistently refused to recognise guerrillas as soldiers; on the same day on which the Partisan Ranger Act was passed, Brigadier General James Totten issued Order Number 47, referring to bands of guerrillas as "marauders and murderers" in an effort to put a stop to what was apparently effective guerrilla activity, and adding:

All those found in arms and open opposition to the laws and legitimate authorities, who are known familiarly as guerrillas … will be shot when found perpetuating their foul acts.

The order also called for the arrest and trial by a military commission of those who gave either shelter or sustenance, or both, to guerrillas,[5] but the guerrillas continued to sting, and, on January 20, 1863, General Order Number Three was issued by order of Brigadier General Loan, that called for the execution of any one holding a partisan commission, recruiting guerrilla soldiers, or giving aid of any kind to Confederate soldiers or partisan rangers.[6] Union officers, attempting to deny the military status of partisans, asserted that guerrillas killing men who supported the Union, or assembling to begin a raid, might well come under civil authority for committing acts of manslaughter and unlawful assembly.[7]

Some partisans wore uniforms, and some did not; photographs of Southern guerrilla troopers show a variance from the neat gray uniforms of Colonel John Singleton Mosby's[8] and Colonel Harry Gilmore's[9] Virginian and Marylander Partisan Rangers, to the uniformed and partly-uniformed guerrillas of Captain Quantrill's Regiment, to fierce-looking armed men in civilian dress.[10] Texan Partisans supplied all of their own gear and weapons, and their uniforms consisted of civilian clothes or loose battle shirts of flannel or twill; Arizonan Rangers who mustered into the Confederate Army in August, 1861, "were described as 'scruffy frontiersmen' who bore little resemblance to an organized military force."[12] Phillip Haythornthwaite, who published an illustrated book in England about Civil War uniforms, commented about the dress of "guerrillas and bushwackers" with these words:

> Wearing a garb of the coarsest texture of homespun linen or linsey-woolsey, tattered and torn ... a dilapidated hat or cap of some wild animal covering his head ... his feet covered with moccasins.

Haythornthwaite found this "uniform" in Virginia, not the Far West.[13] It is undoubtedly true that such lack of military dress contributed to the lack of recognition of guerrillas as soldiers.

Not all Confederate officers approved of partisan warfare, and Robert E. Lee, who felt guerrillas had a negative effect on regular troops, only reluctantly tolerated Mosby's status as a partisan ranger.[14] The Partisan Ranger Act was repealed on February 17, 1864, but the repeal bill allowed rangers, currently serving with regular cavalry units, to continue that service, and thereafter be considered regulars, not partisan rangers. Bands of partisan rangers were encouraged to unite and form battalions and regiments "with the view to bringing them under the general conditions of the provisional army as to discipline, control, and movements ... "The Repeal Act, nonetheless, exempted "such companies as are serving within the lines of the enemy ..."[15] That exemption, of course, applied to any band operating in California and the other parts of the Far West.

Partisans, especially in the West, did not present a military appearance, did nasty deeds which often crossed the line of civil law, and inflicted effective harassment on the enemy; it was a different kind of war that many professional military officers had difficulty in accepting. The foregoing is mentioned to put into perspective the irregular military forces which fought in California during the war. The Californian partisan rangers and guerrilla bands should not be consigned to the category of outlaws; they operated as partisans of both sides were operating in other states.

The men about to be described did espouse the Southern War for Independence; although they were charged with outlawry by the civil and military authorities, the official records bear witness that the Federals in California knew whom they were fighting. In one of numerous letters which appear in those records, Lieutenant Colonel William Jones, the commanding officer of Camp Babbit at Visalia, California, wrote to R. C. Drum, Assistant Adjutant General, Department of the Pacific, on August 6, 1863, informing him that a Sergeant Strobel of Company I, Second California Volunteer Cavalry, had been shot and killed by a "noted rebel," who escaped, and that an outbreak could be looked for at any moment, for the "rebels are well organised." Jones had issued arms to Union irregulars, and appealed for more arms for that purpose. On August 16, Jones informed Drum he was convinced there would be an attack upon the camp, and the guerrillas would receive aid from Fresno.[16]

Jones's correspondence is valid evidence that he did not combat simple Californian outlaws hopeful of loot; the pressure on Camp Babbit by guerrillas was not an isolated instance, for, in some parts of California, especially the Santa Clara Valley, Visalia, Sonoma, and southern California in general, there were strong groups of secessionists. Shipments of gold, silver, and stores were confiscated in the name of the Confederacy by armed irregulars, and sympathisers in southern California persevered in attempts to smuggle these to the Confederacy, and, at the same time, to sabotage shipments intended for Union forces. Guerrillas attacked carriers of gold bullion, and stirred up trouble with Indians and native Californians of Mexican descent.[17]

One of the more notable of these bands was Captain Rufus Henry Ingram's Partisan Rangers, and another was George Belt's guerrilla band, led by "Mason and Henry." Unlike partisans such as Cole Younger, Frank James, Kit Dalton, John Mosby, and Harry Gilmore, California's guerrillas wrote no memoirs; all that is known of them comes from the pens of their enemies.

On June 30, 1864, between 9 P. M. and 10 P. M., on the narrow grade about two and one-half miles above Sportsman's Hall near Placerville, the two coaches of the Pioneer Stage Line were stopped by six men, who, armed with shotguns and pistols, took eight sacks of bullion from the coaches; they did not rob the passengers, and stated all they wanted was the treasure box of Wells, Fargo, & Co. Before leaving, the captain of the band handed one of the drivers a receipt for the confiscated treasure, written as follows:

This is to certify that I have received from Wells, Fargo, & Co., the sum of $ ____ cash, for the purpose of outfitting recruits enlisted in California for the Confederate States Army.
R. Henry Ingram.
Captain, Com'g Co., C. S. A. June, 1864.[18]

Without question, one of the most daring and desperate undertakings by any members of California's secessionist movement was the organisation of a band of Confederate guerrilla by Captain Rufus Ingram and Thomas Bell Poole, the former undersheriff of Monterey County; Poole was an ardent Democrat and Confederate sympathiser, who was quick to join the Knights of the Golden Circle when the War began, and participated with Asbury Harpending, his fellow Kentuckian, in the attempt to turn the *Chapman* into a Confederate privateer. When that endeavour failed, Tom Poole and other crewmen were charged with treason and imprisoned at Alcatraz to await trial, being held seven months, but released in October, 1863, on the condition they take the oath of allegiance and post a $3,000 bond; Poole took the oath, but had little intention of keeping it, for he was always ready to join in any effort to aid the Confederacy, and removed to San Jose, where he joined the local chapter of the Knights of the Golden Circle.[19]

Early in 1864, Rufus Henry Ingram, a 30-year-old former member of William C. Quantrill's guerrilla company, began attending the meetings; he was a medium-sized, heavily bearded, well-educated, and well-mannered man with a magnetic personality, who had left the Missouri guerrillas, and was traveling in Mexico, where he met George Baker, a young farmer from San Jose then on his way to join the Confederate Army. Ingram, whose brother John also lived at San Jose, learned from Baker that there were others like himself in the Santa Clara Valley ready to fight for the South, but, as in the rest of the state, they lacked leadership; Ingram convinced Baker to return with him to California to recruit soldiers for the Confederacy.

Laurence F. Talbott, PhD

Ingram and Baker met with the Knights of the Golden Circle at San Jose; Ingram presented his commission as a captain in the Confederate Army, and explained he wanted to lead a party of men to the Southern states to fight. Many of the Knights agreed to join his band, and Ingram picked Tom Poole as his lieutenant; some of the others who joined Ingram were the captain's brother, John Ingram, John and Wallace Clendenning, John Creal Bouldware, a carpenter of San Jose, James Wilson, a young blacksmith from Missouri, Henry I. Jarboe, Joseph W. Gamble, Washington Jordan, John Gately, Thomas and James Frears, and George Cross, a well-known pioneer who had come to California with John Fremont, taken part in the Bear Flag Revolt, and made a small fortune panning for gold in 1848. Preston Hodges allowed members of the band to camp near his ranch, and provided them with food and horses; John A. Robinson, a shopkeeper of San Jose, also joined the group, and recruited his 18-year-old clerk, Alban H. Glasby, who had arrived in California from Missouri the year before. The only criminal of the entire guerrilla unit was Jim Grant, born in Ireland and raised in Tennessee, where he had been a horse thief; he had killed two men in a drunken brawl before arriving at San Jose.[20]

These men formed the nucleus of a band that became known as "Captain Ingram's Partisan Rangers." Ingram appeared frequently at meetings of the Knights, and attempted to raise funds to equip his men for the trip to the South, but money was scarce, and he was unable to obtain the needed financing, yet, knowing that large shipments of gold were being sent over the road from the Comstock Lode to Sacramento, he decided to activate some of his command, and seize his financing from gold-bearing stages.

After May 1, 1864, most of the Rangers made their headquarters at Hodges' Ranch. Jim Grant, the desperado, had proved too talkative during his frequent drinking bouts, and quarrelled with two other Rangers, threatening to kill them; the resulting tumult caused Ingram to feel Grant would ruin his entire operation, and so he discharged him from the company.[21]

On June 21, Captain Ingram assembled five of his Rangers, including Tom Poole, to ride to Placerville, and, on the afternoon of June 27, Ingram and his party arrived at Somerset House, about 13 miles south of Placerville; on June 30, the Rangers rode to a bend in the highway about 11 miles east, where they remained concealed until dark, talking about their plan, and agreed to fight to the last if attacked, and never be taken prisoner, for the partisans were determined to resist anybody who sought to arrest them. As military commander, Captain Ingram would give a receipt for the gold, believing that Union military guards would be their adversaries.

Two stagecoaches left Virginia City that morning, with 14 passengers each and several sacks of gold and silver bullion; it was 10 o'clock that night when the stages were stopped by the partisan rangers.[22] The story of the taking of the bullion is best told by the testimony of Charles Watson, the driver of the second stage, and the first witness called in the trial of Preston Hodges:

On the first of July last, I was living in Placerville and driving stage; on the night of the 30th. of June, we were coming down the Strawberry, and the stage ahead of me was stopped and robbed of three sacks of bullion; I recognised two of the parties concerned in the robbery, Pool[sic] and Glasby; the first I saw of Pool on the night we were robbed, he was passing by Glasby, who was standing with two pistols cocked and presented on me; all the parties were armed: one had a shotgun; before this, a shot had been fired at them from the first coach; they were excited and came back somewhat enraged; I had to talk good to get along with them; someone snapped a pistol; I don't know who; I got down off the coach and went up to about twelve feet of the front coach when I met a man with a shotgun who told me to stop or he would put a hole in me; I went back; they came up to me and told me to hand out the bullion and Wells, Fargo, & Co.'s treasure box.

Apparently, Watson thought he might be able to outwit the rangers, because he tried to hold back some of the shipment, a stratagem which might have succeeded, had not one of the Rangers been careful. Watson's testimony continued:

I handed out the bullion, but kept the treasure box in, thinking they might not find it; they asked me if that was all the bullion; I said, "Yes," one of them said, "No; I want to see if he has it all out." Did not like to take my word for it; he reached over and took the treasure box; I told him he ought not to take it; he asked why, and I replied that it was from Genoa, and there was little or nothing in it.

The mention of Genoa as the origin of the trip was an attempt to indicate that there was no valuable cargo; Genoa is a small Mormon community, south of Carson City. As Watsons' testimony shews, the ruse did not work:

He said, if there was nothing in it, he would leave it the next day where I could get it; I asked what they expected to do with that much bullion;

they said they were going to raise an army for the Southern Confederacy; they gave me a receipt to that effect; would know that receipt if I saw it again; they must have taken two hundred and fifty pounds of bullion; there were two bars in one of the sacks; I think what they took in all must have been worth $20,000; there were some $20,000 in the treasure box in coin and dust.

Some accounts of the robbery say that the rangers were masked; others have said Ingram wore the uniform of a Confederate captain. Watson made no mention of either, and seemed to have had no difficulty in recognising the participants of the holdup. Watson continued:

Glasby held two pistols, pointed at me; I asked him to hold them down, as they might go off; am certain I saw a weapon in Pool's hands; there were six persons in all around the stage; when they asked me to throw the bullion out, I said I had no one to hold the horses; they replied, there was a man to hold them; and I saw one at the head of the horses; they said they were going to get soldiers for the Southern Army; this took place about ten o'clock at night; eleven or twelve miles from Somerset House.[23]

The guerrillas buried the bullion, and rode back to Somerset House for breakfast and sleep. Two members of the *posse* from Placerville tracked them to the house, and a gun battle ensued, in which Constable Joseph Staples was killed, and Constable George Ranney was badly wounded.

Tom Poole had sustained a facial wound, and so the guerrillas rode away, leaving him to await a buggy that they promised to send for him. The Placerville sheriff and his *posse* arrived first, about noon, after the guerrillas had already attained a six-hour start; the life of the wounded constable was saved by a doctor who rode with the *posse*. Poole was arrested, and taken to the Placerville gaol, where he recovered from his wounds. The *posse* lost the trail of the guerrillas, and turned back to Placerville. Ingram's men rode to Fresno County, where they were able to be resupplied by allies amongst the population; at Placerville, Tom Poole is reported, by one account, to have made a full confession, but other accounts deny that he did.

Still seeking more financing through friends of San Jose, Ingram learnt that a large payroll for the New Almaden Mines would be collected there on the afternoon of July 15, 1864, on the evening of which Captain Ingram, Baker, John Clendenning, John Bouldware, and Glasby gathered to the Almaden Road, about a mile from San Jose, where they remained overnight. That afternoon, a careless remark made to a rancher, who lived nearby, made the rancher aware of the plan to steal the payroll; he contrived to slip away and inform a neighbour, who, in turn, reported the planned attack to the sheriff of Santa Clara County. The guerrillas were waiting in a small whitewashed building, set back from the road, and surrounded by brush and trees, which was surrounded by the posse, who called for the Confederates to surrender; at the posse's demand, a battle ensued, with each of the guerrillas moving outside with two revolvers firing. Forty shots were exchanged at close range; a deputy sheriff was wounded twice, and John Clendenning was wounded by a shotgun blast, but able to disappear into the brush. One of Al Glasby's pistols jammed, and the other was destroyed by fire from the *posse*; seven bullet holes were found in his clothing when he surrendered. John Bouldware traded fire with two *posse* men, and was seriously wounded, but kept firing until he was overpowered by two men: he still did not give up his pistols, until the barrel of a gun was put in his ear. He died almost immediately, still struggling.

Captain Ingram and George Baker shot their way to freedom in the surrounding thickets. The *posse* returned to San José with the body of John Bouldware and their prisoner, Glasby; Clendenning was found later in the afternoon, fatally wounded, and died in the San José gaol.

Young Glasby was frightened enough to name the rest of the Partisan Rangers, whom the Union military apparently recognised as soldiers, because four companies of Union infantry were sent with the civil law enforcement officers in order to capture the men Glasby had named, warrants for whose arrest were issued at Placerville, although the arrests were eventually made by Union forces in Santa Clara County. On July 29, Preston Hodges, John Ingram, Wallace Glendenning, George Cross, Henry Jarboe, Joseph Gamble, John Gately, John Robinson, and the Frear brothers were taken prisoner, and brought to Placerville, where they joined Glasby and Poole in gaol: neither Captain Ingram nor George Baker were ever captured. Authorities believed that they had fled to Missouri to join Confederate guerrillas still fighting there.

Preston Hodges was convicted of second-degree murder, but the conviction was overturned by the Supreme Court on the grounds his action as an accessory had not taken place in El Dorado County; Hodges and all of the others, with the exception of Poole, were sent to San José, where Hodges was re-convicted of treason and murder as an accessory in the death of the lawman killed at Somerset House. Glasby was released for turning state's evidence, and the rest of the band, except Poole, had the charges of murder dismissed, for the evidence against them "was of a vague and untenable nature."

Laurence F. Talbott, PhD

Thomas Bell Poole was the only partisan ranger to be convicted and punished. His case was a strange one: first, Poole had never been an outlaw, but was a former undersheriff of Monterey County, a six-foot, rough-looking Kentucky widower who had raised several children on his ranch in the Pajaro Valley. He was a devout Southern patriot, had been the only prisoner taken when he was wounded at Somerset House, and was in gaol at the time when the rangers had fought their last battle, nor had he, as a ranger, killed anyone. Tom Poole's trial for murder began on August 24, 1864, at Placerville, less than two months after the Wells, Fargo, & Co. robbery, or, as the rangers viewed their act, confiscation; even though he had not pulled the trigger, he was, by law, a principal in the deputy's death.

Glasby testified against his fellow guerrillas in a trial which lasted three days, at which the jury deliberated for a mere fifteen minutes before returning the verdict of guilty; the conviction was appealed to the California Supreme Court, but upheld. Poole's many friends, and many prominent citizens of Monterey and El Dorado Counties, requested clemency; those who sought to stop Poole's execution included the Sheriff of Placerville and seven members of the jury which had convicted him. The former judge, James Johnson, a friend of Poole's, pleaded with Governor Frederick Low: "Do not the hundreds of thousands of Southern men slain sufficiently atone for the Southern rebellion? Has not enough blood been shed? Shall Poole be executed, and Lee, Bragg, and Joe Johnston go at large?"

Governor Low was not influenced; of the six men involved in the fight at Somerset House where the deputy had been killed, two had been shot to death, two had escaped, and one had turned state's evidence, leaving Poole alone to be punished. On September 29, 1865, Poole, smiling and cordial, shook hands with his gaolers, and then mounted the scaffold where he retained his composure throughout his execution.

Poole never considered himself a criminal, but a prisoner of war, saying, "We did not think of being arrested by the civil authorities; we expected it to be a regular fight, the same as in the Atlantic States. If we were taken, we would be treated as prisoners of war." He had a point. Ingram's company had been recognised as a Confederate unit by the Union press, and Federal infantry had participated in the capture of the main body of the company, yet, five months after Appomattox, a Confederate soldier was reluctantly hanged by a civilian executioner.[24]

The manner in which partisans were regarded and treated in California was not unique to that state, for, as it was mentioned earlier, Confederate partisan soldiers were often treated as criminals by their Northern captors.

Throughout the records of the Southern partisans who fought in the Northern states, the captured partisans were charged with treason and murder, and often executed, even though they were enlisted members of the armed forces of the Confederate States.[25]

The press of the North were particularly vindictive towards partisans. The San Francisco *Alta California* wrote an editorial about Ingram's hold-up, entitled, "Ingraham [sic] and His Highwaymen," and "Details of the Late Robbery, or Cut-Throat Raid by Ingraham and His Gang," in which such things as the following were written:

It has been impossible until now to get a correct version of the gang, the doings of the gang, their objects, &c., as neither of the two (Glasby and Poole) that are now in our gaol have made a "clean breast" of it.

The leader, Captain Ingraham, is late from Missouri, where he obtained the reputation of a bushwhacker and desperado, and was known as the "Red Fox." He emigrated to California for the purpose of inaugurating a guerrilla warfare, hoping, by meeting with success, to be joined by other organisations made up of the same elements throughout the state, which he informed his men "he expected and had been assured by their friends," and particularly his Santa Clara County friends, to rally to his standard. He exhibited his commission as captain in the service of the C. S. A. to his gang. Glasby says he and the rest of them joined under those representations. Ingraham had no doubt improved his time since coming here in traveling around the state, getting posted and making acquaintances among his stripe. He said he taught school a few months last spring, near Mud Springs, in this County. He had a party made up to rob the express.

If this was the nucleus of an organization, the facts are strongly on that side, around which the secesh rebels of this state were to rally for the purpose of bringing on the people the horrors of a guerrilla warfare.[26]

The Sacramento Union published this editorial on August 29, 1864:

LETTERS FROM PLACERVILLE.
Trial of Thomas B. Pool and others for the murder of Jos. M. Staples, Deputy Sheriff, and for the robbery of Wells, Fargo, & Co.'s Express.

The trial was for murder. Judge S. W. Brockway charged the jury to decide whether Poole, if convicted, was guilty of first, or second, degree murder; no consideration was given to Poole's affiliation with the Confederacy, yet, at its close, the editorial opines:

The audience which had crowded the courtroom for days, appeared to be relieved and greatly satisfied that treason, robbery, and murder had met its reward at the hands of the jury.

The trial of the balance of the conspirators will commence September 5th, when the history of Captain Ingraham's Partisan Rangers will be detailed in full, from Richmond to the Somerset House.[27]

The reference to "treason" and "Richmond," the capital of the Confederacy, would indicate the editor knew the authorities were not trying common criminals, but partisans.

The *Sacramento Union* of September 10, 1864, in its editorial, "Trial of Preston Hodges," acknowledged the receipt signed by R. Henry Ingram, as Captain, C. S. A., offered as evidence of the robbery.[28]

There seems to be something of a mystery in the spirited attack on the Confederate partisan rangers by the *Weekly Mountain Democrat* of Placerville, California, which did not even go as far as the *Sacramento Union* in acknowledging Ingram's company as Confederate partisan rangers. Since the *Mountain Democrat* was Southern in sympathy, and critical of Washington, it would seem logical it might at least acknowledge Ingram's company as guerrillas rather than bandits; a review of earlier numbers of the *Mountain Democrat* has provided a possible answer for the paper's animosity.

The landlady of Somerset House, Maria Reynolds, gave the names and physical descriptions of the partisan rangers who stopped with her before the robbery, and breakfasted with her afterwards; as cited in the *Mountain Democrat*, she described "the villains who robbed the stage, who have yet to be arrested." She gave physical descriptions of John Clendenning, George Baker, John Creal, Ab Gillespie, and Ralph Henry;[29] except for Clendenning and Baker, she had the names wrong. "Ralph Henry" may have been Rufus Henry Ingram. "Gillespie" was probably Alban Glasby, and "John Creal" was probably John Creal Bouldware; it should be noted those of Southern background often include middle names when addressing one another. Some ten days later, she identified them correctly by name, and testified they had arrived at Somerset House about 4 o'clock in the evening, and stayed until morning; later, she asked them who they were, and they told her they were Confederate officers sent to collect money for the Confederate Army.[30]

It is necessary to read the number of the *Mountain Democrat* for January 25, 1862, to find the next clew, in which the paper, in its usual mode of Southern sympathy, editorialised its displeasure over the appointment of James Lane, the U. S. Senator from Kansas, and abolitionist guerrilla chief, as a general in the Federal army, "Authorised to prosecute unconformity with his own notions, unrestricted and unembarrassed by the War Department. How he will conduct the war is not left to conjecture. On his part, it will be a war of devastation, rapine, and murder … God help the unoffending, unprotected who fall into Lane's hands."[31]

The Kansan guerrillas were obviously hated by the editor of the *Mountain Democrat*; ironically, the Somerset House landlady's incorrect report of the names of partisans caused the paper to back away from any support for the partisans, and to challenge their credibility as Confederate soldiers. Her identification of a "John Creal" among them struck a note with the editor, for, when writing of the event, the editor stated John Kreal, one of the Santa Clara robbers, was formerly a Kansas Jayhawker, who had been a pupil of Senator Lane and a lieutenant to him, and further speculated that other of the "outlaws" had similar antecedents,[32] and thus a San Jose carpenter turned partisan ranger, John Creal Bouldware, was misidentified as a Kansas guerrilla lieutenant. This cast suspicion that Captain Ingram's men were common desperados.

The *Mountain Democrat* for August 6, 1864, correctly listed the Rangers brought into Placerville, but, by then, John Creel Bouldware had been killed, and was not named.[33] The claim of the men was they were Confederate soldiers from Missouri operating under the authority of the Confederate government.[34]

The partisan rangers served under a captain commissioned by the Confederate States Army, and were not desperate outlaws, but farmers and tradesmen, trying to serve their country: none of them profited from the gold they took, and it is believed the gold did find its way into Confederate hands. It was never recovered.

Richard H. Dillon's essay, "California's Expeditionary Forces," mentions the skirmish between advance scouts of the Californian column and Captain R. S. Hunter's Confederate Arizona Rangers at Stanwyx Ranch, about eighty miles east of Yuma, was thought to be the westernmost fight of the War; Dillon, however, notes that an exception would be the shootout at Somerset House, "between Confederate irregulars and lawmen."[35] That was indeed a Californian engagement which took place in El Dorado County, but the final shootout that defeated Ingram's Rangers occurred in Santa Clara County, off the Almaden Road, only a mile from San Jose, a city of the East Bay. This was surely the westernmost combat involving a Confederate military unit, irregular or not.

Laurence F. Talbott, PhD

NOTES TO CHAPTER X.

1. Leslie, Edward E. *The Devil Knows How To Ride*. Random House. New York. 1996. pp. 83-192.
2. Leslie, pp. 83-192.
3. Steele, Phillip, and Steve Cottrell. *Civil War in the Ozarks*. Pelican Publishing Company. Gretna. 1994. p. 50.
4. Teel, Robert W. *Cullen Montgomery Baker: Champion of the Lost Cause*. Robert W. Teel. Huntsville. 1995. p. 30.
5. Leslie, pp. 119-120.
6. United States War Department. *The War of the Rebellion: A Compilation of the Official Records of the Union and Confederate Armies*. p. 66.
7. O. R. Series I. Vol. XXII. Pt. 2. p. 50.
8. Siepel, Kevin H. *Rebel*. St Martins Press. New York. 1983. pp. 68-69.
9. Gilmore, Colonel Harry. *Four Years in the Saddle*. Harper & Brothers. New York. 1866. pp. 2-12.
10. Steele and Cattell, pp. 61, 115, 117.
11. Frazier, Donald S. *Blood and Treasure*. Texas A. & M. University Press. College Station. 1995. pp. 30, 132.
12. Finch, L. Boyd. *Confederate Pathway to the Pacific*. The Arizona Historical Society. Tucson. 1996. pp. xiv-xv, 82.
13. Haythornthwaite, Philip J. *Uniforms of the American Civil War*. Blandford Press. Dorset. England. 1975. p. 133.
14. O. R. Series I. Vol. XIV. p. 581. O.R. Series I. Vol. XII. Pt. 3. p. 899.
15. O. R. Series I. Vol. III. p. 194.
16. O. R. Series I. Vol. L. Pt. 2. p. 572.
17. Fitzgibbons, Margaret. *History of the United Daughters of the Confederacy*. Blue Bird Publishing. Mesa. 1997. pp. 431, 442.
18. Gilbert, Benjamin Franklin. "San Francisco Harbour Defence During the Civil War." *California Historical Society Quarterly*. Vol. 33. N° 3. September, 1954. p. 234.
19. *Historical Souvenir of El Dorado County, California*. Paolo Sioli. Oakland. 1883. pp. 150-151.
20. Boessenecker, John. *Badge and Buckshot*. University of Oklahoma Press. Norman. 1987. pp. 133-136.
21. Boessenecker, pp. 137-138.
22. Boessenecker, pp. 138-140.
23. "The Placerville Highwaymen." "Trial of Preston Hodges." *Sacramento Daily Union*. September 9, 1864. p. 1.
24. *Sacramento Daily Union*. September 9, 1864. p. l.

25. Headley, John W. *Confederate Operations in Canada and New York.* Neale Publishing Company. New York. 1906. pp. 19,479.
26. "Our Letter From Placerville, Cal." "Ingraham{sic) and His Highwaymen." Editorial. *Alta California.* July 27, 1864. p. 2.
27. "Letter from Placerville." "Trial of Thomas B. Pool [sic] and Others for the Murder of Jos. M. Staples, Deputy Sheriff, and for the Robbery of Wells, Fargo, & Co.'s Express." Editorial. *Sacramento Union.* August 29, 1864. p. 2.
28. "Trial of Preston Hodges." *Sacramento Union.* September 9, 1864. p. l.
29. "Description of the Stage Robbers." *Weekly Mountain Democrat.* July 16, 1864. p. 2.
30. *Alta California.* July 27, 1864. p. 2.
31. *Mountain Democrat.* January 25, 1862. N°.4.p. 2.
32. *Mountain Democrat.* July 28, 1864. p. 2.
33. *Mountain Democrat.* August 6, 1864. p. 2.
34. *Mountain Democrat.* July 23, 1864. p. 2.
35. Dillon, Richard H. "California's Expeditionary Forces." Salvo: *Journal of the Fort Point and Army Museum Association.* Vol. 6. N° 4. Spring, 1990. p. 24.

The Battle of Valverde. Painting by Olga Vatz,
reproduced by courtesy of the artist.

CHAPTER XI.
GUERRILLAS.

Whereas the Partisan Rangers organised in the Santa Clara Valley by Captain Rufus Henry Ingram may well have come under the Partisan Ranger Act of 1862, passed by the Confederate Congress, the guerrilla band that became known as the Mason and Henry Gang probably had no such recognition; this band seems to have operated much the same as the Southern guerrilla bands that, like their Union counterparts, ravaged Missouri and Kansas. As was the situation in Missouri, where the Southern guerrillas were considered patriots and defenders by much of the population, Mason and Henry apparently had popular support within Fresno and Tulare Counties, and the aiding and abetting of those engaged in the Southern cause was strongly condemned by a most vociferous pro-union newspaper, the *Visalia Delta*.

Most of the population of the southern San Joaquin Valley were former residents of the Southern states, a majority of whom supported the secession of the eleven states that formed the Confederacy; belief in the righteousness of the South was often quite outspoken by many, including some prominent citizens. Even Colonel Thomas Baker, the founder of Bakersfield, and then a senator, was accused of being a supporter of the Confederate States, and, in 1862, was detained at Camp Babbit at Visalia, established for the sole purpose of controlling the surrounding population during the War.

The Mason and Henry band of guerrillas operated in the Tejon Canyon area, as perhaps did others of their kind. Captain Moses McLaughlan, U. S. A., wrote: "The decision of the Army to close down Fort Tejon in 1861 was wrong. … Tactically, the fort was necessary to help contain large segments of population in the San Joaquin Valley which were sympathetic to the Confederacy."

Lieutenant Colonel William Jones, U. S. A., echoed Captain McLaughlan's opinion, stating: "If there is any part of this state (California) that should be patrolled, it is the southern tier of counties, for there is no county in the state that offers such facilities for the organisation of lawless bands of thieves and outlaws, and there is no county on earth that can furnish more or better material, according to its inhabitants, than this tier of counties can for purposes of this kind."[1]

Out of the mostly unorganised hostility Federal forces encountered in parts of California, the Mason and Henry guerrilla band was born and sustained. The years of 1863 and 1864 have been considered violent ones in the valley, but Mason and Henry, who were often accused of various crimes during that time, were not organised until the summer of 1864.

The *Visalia Times Delta*, in its "Golden Century Edition" of 1959, stated, in March, 1863, a series of crimes began, involving the robbing and killing of an express driver by masked men, the murder of a teamster and the proprietor of a stage line, and other misdeeds; the proprietor of the stage line was generally believed to have been killed by Indians, but the Mason and Henry gang "came to be suspected of committing this series of criminal acts," a supposition which could not, of course, possibly be correct. The article goes on to state "the county's (Kern) first badmen were real enough, although they remain in some respects figures of mystery."[2] The historian of Kern County, William Harland Boyd, wrote, because members of the Mason and Henry band operated outside the law, they became "scapegoats" for much of the lawlessness of the time, and it is difficult to determine what specific "crimes" they did commit.[3] The many notions and indictments of Mason and Henry, often emotional and contradictory, are worth examination in the attempt to discover the truth about a rather rough and dirty area of the history of the War in California.

Amongst those hostile to the Federal government's occupation of the San Joaquin Valley was the owner of a large ranch on the Merced River, who was a strong secessionist, and wanted to wage guerrilla warfare against "Unionmen" and Union troops.[4] He was George G. Belt, a former Alcalde of Stockton, an Indian trader, and a very wealthy man. A native of Maryland, Belt was characterised as being a "fiery Southerner," and, accompanying his interest in forming a Confederate guerrilla force, he was also interested in the notion of a Pacific Republic, in the event that the war for Southern independence should fail.[5]

George Belt began to outfit his guerrilla "army" after he met the two hardened men who would be its leaders. How he met them is unknown; the two were very unlikely companions for a prominent former judge and large rancher.

The first, Thomas McCauley, was born in Illinois about 1833, and came to California with his brother Edward during the early 1850s; he was described by an early writer as a "large strong fellow, a rough of pronounced type, whose occupation, if he had any, beyond quarrelling and fighting, is not known." The McCauleys settled in Tuolumne County, and, with some hard-drinking associates, became outlaws. Edward McCauldey was hanged for murder, and Thomas sentenced to prison; however, by 1863, he was free, and had resided in Merced and Fresno Counties, where he may have remained an outlaw. Outlaw or not, he took the name of

James Henry to cover his past.[6]

John Mason was working as a hostler at Fort Tejon in 1860; he is reported to have used the name, John J. Malone, which could have been his real name. Mason and Henry met in the spring of 1864, and it is said that, when they met, both were on the run, but why or from what or whom is not known; they were both working on a ranch in the San Joaquin Valley where they became friends, and it was shortly afterwards that they met George Belt.

It was upon his meeting with Mason and Henry that Belt offered to support the Confederate guerrilla band if they were able to form one. Belt probably had little knowledge of the past of his captains, but was undoubtedly aware of and appreciated their ferocity;[7] that was important if they were to carry out the mission which they were to be given, namely, to kill every Union man in the valley in order to start a revolution that would separate California from the Union.[8] Recruiting began during the summer of 1864, in the face of a severe drought, and the bad war news from the South.[9]

There was apparently little, if any, success in the recruitment of guerrilla fighters in the Santa Clara Valley during the summer of 1864; it has been stated in at least one source that Mason and Henry gave up their mission from George Belt and turned to a life of crime,[10] but, when the actual deeds of the band are carefully studied, there is no evidence the Southern cause was abandoned until well after the end of the War.

Although Henry was a native of Illinois, Mason was from the South, and eager to fight for the Southern cause; because of the Southern sympathy of much of the Valley's population, there were constant rumours of operations of the kind that Belt organised. The privateer incident that involved Asbury Harpending, and the robbery at Sportsman's Hall by Captain Rufus Henry Ingram's Confederate Partisan Rangers, gave credence to such rumours.[11]

Another prominent citizen of Kern County who was an associate of Belt's guerrilla band was John Gordon, a businessman of Tailhort, a settlement later known as White River, suspected by some as being the "brains" of the band, who supplied facilities a few miles from his residence, including a large cave near the mines of Grizzly Gulf that provided an enclosed hiding place large enough to conceal men and their horses, an ideal retreat.[12]

Mason and Henry did successfully recruit a guerrilla band; though the number of the members of the band may not have been large by military standards, it was reported, during one action, to have consisted of twenty

Laurence F. Talbott, PhD

men.[13] By April, 1866, thirty-five warrants had been issued against the members.[14]

Accounts, including those from the *Visalia Delta*, leave little doubt that Mason and Henry fought against "Union men" and the United States Army in the San Joaquin Valley; the reports which appeared in the *Visalia Delta* are probably the best primary source available on the activities of the guerrilla band throughout their existence. As stated earlier, the *Delta* was a strongly pro-union publication, with editorials which are quite revealling, regarding the political motivation of the guerrillas, and its accounts of Mason and Henry are somewhat like the adventures of Robin Hood as they might have been written by the Sheriff of Nottingham: nevertheless, much insight regarding Mason and Henry is contained on the *Delta's* pages. It may be of interest to recall that the pro-Southern newspaper, the Visalia *Equal Rights Expositor,* had its printing press destroyed by a mob of Federal soldiers from Camp Babbit in March, 1863,[15] and it would undoubtedly be quite interesting to know what that publication would have printed from 1864 to 1865 in regard to partisan and guerrilla action.

The first Mason and Henry attack on a Union man took place about midnight on November 8, 1864. Mason and Henry rode to Hawthorne's Stage Station, west of Visalia, and called the owner to the door, where Mason shot and killed him without warning. "You'll be questioned about this," Mason told several stage hands, "Tell them that I killed him. I, John Mason, and tell them I did, it for he was a damned Black Republican, had voted for Lincoln, and must die." The following morning they killed E. G. Robinson as he was returning from voting.

Governor Low issued a proclamation on November 14, 1864, offering $500 each for the capture of any of the guerrillas;[16] the *Visalia* Delta, in its number of November 23; 1864, published a notice that Governor Low had offered a reward of $1,000 for Mason and Henry, and that, if "our detectives or somebody else" would furnish a description of the fugitives, the paper would gladly publish it."[17] The offer was apparently accepted, and the number of November 30 carried a full description of both Mason and Henry, quite detailed, but additional information followed that had been submitted to the paper after the initial descriptions had been put in print; the descriptions were of two rough-looking characters, and included their height, weight, habitual dress, horses, equipment, and weapons.[18] There was nothing unusual for the times, and neither man was of imposing size.

The same number contained a copy of a letter from the Sheriff of Fresno county, J. Scott Ashman, to the Sheriff of Tulare County, John Gill, dated November 25, 1864, which had been sent from Firebaugh's Ferry, and was headlined, "Pursuit of the 'Peace Democrat Murderers' Mason and Henry;" the letter recounts the Fresno sheriff's attempt to apprehend the Mason and Henry Gang. Sheriff Ashman left Millertown on November 17, and, on the 18th, arrived at an unnamed spot, where he heard from a stage driver that Mason and Henry were supposed to be in Moody Canyon in the Coast Range, about forty miles away; Ashman wrote he and three others in his posse followed the fugitives, and were later joined by eleven men from the lower King's River who were on the same mission, and that the larger group was "very poorly prepared." The combined *posse* began their journey on November 21, and arrived at their destination on the 23rd, adding that all but three of his party were on foot, and that the horses were tired. At about 8 o'clock in the morning, smoke was sighted on the summit of the mountain, now about three miles away; as the fourteen men started for the fire, they found that the tracks of their quarry, two horses and a dog, had been joined by those of two more horsemen, and that the four riders had started south, following the summit of the mountain. The three mounted members of the *posse* followed, and came close enough to the four guerrillas for Ashman later to describe the four horses in detail, and include in his description that they were followed by a small red dog.

Ashman's letter continues, telling that the three of them considered themselves outnumbered, apparently by one guerrilla and one dog, and returned to the remaining members of the *posse*: Ashman wrote that the entire *posse* felt compelled to "return without accomplishing anything. ... We were out of provisions and horse feed. ... I am very fearful that the 'boys' can not do much in that part of the country."[19]

The *Delta* of November 30, 1864, also carried a notice from the governor of California, dated November 14, 1864, under the heading, "$500 Reward," in which some specific charges are enumerated, such as, "I have received satisfactory evidence that, on or about the 9th instant, a man by the name of Robinson, one by the name of Hawthorne, and another whose name is unknown to me, were brutally murdered in the counties of Tulare and Fresno, and that John Doe, alias Jackson or Miller, and John Mason are the parties who committed the murders."[20]

The editor of the *Visalia Delta* was outraged by, and suspicious of, Sheriff Ashman's retreat from his quarry on November 23, as explained in Ashman's letter to John Gill, expressed in a stinging editorial under "Local News" in the *Delta* for December 24, 1864, wherein it was made clear that the paper believed the Mason and Henry band were Confederate guerrillas, and that the reason why they had not been caught was the Southern sympathy in the area, which possibly included that of Sheriff Ashman. The editor raged: "We are heartily sick and tired of hearing, talking, and writing of the grand force being enacted for the pursuit of Mason and Henry, the murderers of Union men, because they were such by their rebel friends and sympathisers … the faith we felt from the beginning in the honesty of Scott Ashman's intention to capture these marauding democrats … has dwindled down to 'point no point,' and referred to an advertisement directly below the editorial, which offered $1,000 in gold coin of the United States for the capture "of John Monroe, and James Henry, the murderers of Charles Anderson, Joseph Hawthorne, and E. G. Robinson on the 8th and 9th of November 1864, in the county of Fresno," and was signed, J. Scott Ashman, Sheriff, December 14, 1864. The editor commented: "Notwithstanding this and other offers of the same sort."

The editor continued to condemn Sheriff Ashman, saying that the most incredulous would be taxed to believe "that he or any of his kind" really wish to capture the guerrillas, because, amongst them, were the sheriff's political, and probably personal, friends. Based on "information of unquestionable authority," the editor wrote that the three horsemen who came within sight of the "red handed assassins" included two Union men who returned to the main body of the posse, and reported their success to Sheriff Ashman, who, rather than closing on the guerrillas, "as would have been the case had he been in earnest," decided that his party were not prepared for combat, and returned home.

It was the opinion of the editor that, had it been "Peace Democrats" who had been murdered by Union men, the sheriff would have waited overnight, and, when the guerrillas broke camp, then urged his men forward "by their love of humanity, of God, and their hopes of heaven; to persevere at the risk of life and all." Such would have been his language if he had been "thoroughly in earnest in his work."

The editor wrote that, from the facts of the case, it must be concluded "that the whole crew of partisan sympathisers of Peace Democrats of Fresno are participants in the killing of Robinson, Hawthorne, and others, for no wrong they have done, but simply and solely that they voted for Abraham Lincoln, and not for McClellan and Jeff Davis."[21] "The others" mentioned by the editor, "and another" listed in the governor's offer of a reward, appear to be one Charles Anderson alone. The *Delta* identifies all three as Union men, and the editorial of December 21, 1864, certainly indicates Mason and Henry were partisan in those whom they killed; the editor does not mention plunder, only the assassination of Union men and support of the Peace Democrat candidate in the election of November, 1864, together with fealty to the president of the Confederate states, Jefferson Davis. The editor also revealed his frustration that the guerrilla band had community support that he believed to include the Sheriff of Fresno County.

The records indicate that the guerrillas were organised during the summer of 1864, and went into action during the presidential election of that year, when the contending political parties were the Union Party, with Abraham Lincoln as their candidate, and the Peace Democrats, with General George McClellan as theirs: the Union party would continue the war, but the Peace Democrats would make peace with the South. It is not difficult to comprehend the motivation of the guerrillas in November, 1864. As at December, 1864, the three assassinations of Union men were apparently the sole crimes for which the guerrillas were wanted.

The first two months of 1865 may have been a period of recruitment by the guerrilla band; by March, Mason and Henry had recruited some additional followers. Sundry unidentified robberies in the Kern River Valley and the region of San Bernardino were charged to them, and they were pursued by army units who reported that the band consisted of twenty members; very few of their names are recorded, but they include "Texas" John Rogers, Thomas Hawkins, and Joe Dye.[22]

The next specific report of the guerrillas is to be found in the *Visalia Delta* for March 15, 1865, in which skirmishes between the guerrilla band and soldiers from Camp Babbitt were reported. A squad of soldiers had been sent by Captain Noble, under the command of Sergeant Rowley, "in pursuit of the 'Constitutional Democratic' murderers of Union men."

The squad returned after a "very hard skirmish," having traveled more than 900 miles of desolate country for twenty-five days; they reported, after they had left Fort Tejon, they had followed the guerrillas, and finally found them at Sonora, but that they, in the manner of Sheriff Ashman, had been compelled to return because of "their horses giving out and their inability to get new ones."[23] The soldiers of the United States Army involved in the action were a squad from the Second California Cavalry, Company E, Captain Herman Noble, Commanding.[24]

The army reported the guerrillas were well financed, having $3,000 or more in gold in their possession; no source of the wealth was revealed. If it had come from robberies, the *Delta* would not have been reluctant to report the crimes, but, according to the *Delta*, it was believed by many the band had gone to seek more recruits "to return to prey on the lower part of the state, on Union men," the editorial commenting that "they could have obtained plenty of recruits nigher home. Doubtless Visalia would have furnished several birds of prey, and a surgeon or two, to bind up their broken heads, and, very likely, a chaplain to minister to their bruised souls, and any number of spies, sneaks, and informers."[25]

The above account from the *Delta* records the United States Army as having a running skirmish with Confederate guerrillas in the area of Fort Tejon; it is also quite an enlightening commentary of the sympathies of the population of War time Visalia, including members of the medical profession and the clergy.

The same *Delta* carried an article, dated April 9, from Appomattox Courthouse, stating the terms for the surrender of Lee's Army of Northern Virginia, signed by General U. S. Grant; in the same column, from the headquarters of the Army of Northern Virginia, is a letter, also dated April 9, addressed to Grant, signed by General Robert E. Lee, accepting the terms.[26] The War was essentially over for most of the nation, but some Confederate units continued to fight, and President Abraham Lincoln's assassination outraged the North.

As late as May 24, 1865, Federals in the Trans-Mississippi had to continue to operate against guerrilla bands in the west.[27] The last great battle of the war was fought on May 26, 1865, in Texas, about 15 miles above the Brazos Santiago; ironically, it was a Confederate victory by General J. E. Slaughter.[28] On June 2, 1865, the last large body of Confederate soldiers, under General Kirby Smith, consisting of all Southern troops west of the Mississippi, surrendered.[29]

As with some other guerrilla bands, Mason and Henry continued the fight after Lee's surrender; there seems to be two stages in the activities of the bands after it became apparent the South was fighting a lost cause. Some of the San Joaquin Valley's Southern sympathisers hoped that Mason and Henry would continue a guerrilla war that might lead to the formation of the Pacific Republic George Belt had favoured,[30] and that was the course of action that seems to have been taken: thus, the fighting did not stop in the San Joaquin Valley as hostilities were winding down in the East. This late conflict is well recorded, as is the identification of the combatants.

In a series of footnotes, Hurbert Howe Bancroft states: "In the Tehachapi Valley, a band of Confederate guerrillas occupied themselves in the spring of 1865, robbing Union men of horses and other property, and committing occasional murders. During the first week of May, 1865, the inhabitants of San Bernardino were greatly alarmed by the rumour that, in their vicinity, there were "300 to 700 guerrillas from the Confederate army."³¹ Further concern over the continued fighting is expressed in correspondence contained in the U. S. Government's *Official Records*, in which a letter from Headquarters, District of Southern California, dated April 16, 1865, warns, "that it is probable that the death of the president will hasten preparations of secessionists within the lower counties, who have been organised for months to oppose the government of the United States by force." The letter states that an organisation of secessionists were preparing for action of some kind, and, "Consequently, I to-day dispatched a force of 120 men, under the command of Capt. P. Munday, Fourth California Volunteer Infantry, when relieved at Fort Mojave, should post at Camp Cady for the present."³² Captain Patrick Munday commanded Company K of the Fourth California Infantry.³³

On April 26, 1865, Governor Low wrote Major General McDowell, and enclosed a letter from a civilian, M. M. Wheeler, who resided at Kernsville, to his brother, telling him that they had sent to Visalia for troops to assist them, because, "Since the news of the surrender of Lee's army, and the assassination of Lincoln and Seward, and the surrender of Johnston's army and C. (sic], have reached here, the rebs have been perfectly wild with excitement and rage, and have organised a guerrilla band at Clear Creek, fifteen miles from here, and threaten to annihilate us all."³⁴

A letter of May 12, 1865, to Headquarters, District of Southern California, from the Commander of the Fourth California Infantry, informed Headquarters that the band of secessionists who had appeared in the Tehatchepy (sic) Valley, and stole horses there, had ridden east of the mountain range to the San Bernardino Mountains in the vicinity of Bear Valley, where they had divided, one group going into Lower California through San Diego County, others towards the Colorado River, and still others hiding in the neighbouring valleys. The Fourth California Infantry were waiting to engage them.³⁵ There can be little doubt the guerrillas feared at Kernsville and in the Tehachapi Valley were the Mason and Henry band; the locations and events are a match, and no other guerrilla organisations are known to have existed in that region at that time.

On April 18, 1865, the *Los Angeles Tri-Weekly News* reported a gunfight between Mason and a detachment of Union troops at the head of the Great Panache Valley. Mason had been caught by surprise and wounded; however, he escaped. Another detachment of troops were sent after him;³⁶ this may have been an engagement with the Fourth California Infantry.

Whether or not Mason and Henry shared the impossible dream that some of their supporters had of fighting California into a Pacific Republic, wanted to continue their way of life, or simply had no way of surrendering and surviving, is not known; it is well recorded that, for whatever reason, the raiding continued.

On July 13, 1865, two men, who were tentatively identified as Mason and Henry, although Mason's companion was actually Thomas Hawkins, rode into Jewett's Sheep Ranch on the Kern River, and threatened the life of its owner, Philo Jewett, who escaped, and, whilst in hiding, heard a gunshot; a short time later, he called some Indians who belonged to the camp to join him, and returned to the house, where he found John Johnson, his herdsman, dead, shot directly through the body, "and stabbed in the back and breast." Some containers in the house had been broken open, but all that had been taken was two rifles.

Word was sent to Bakersfield; Deputy Sheriff Chapman formed a *posse* of citizens and two Indians, and began pursuit of the killers. The *posse* saw their quarry enter a deep bushy canyon "where they could not be approached without almost certain death to the assaulting party." The *posse* occupied a pass through which, they believed, the killers would attempt to escape; however, Mason and Hawkins successfully escaped by some other route.[37]

Sometime in 1865, members of the guerrilla band had approached Colonel Baker to enlist his aid in killing James Skiles, an ardent Union man; apparently, Philo Jewett also was a Union man.[38]

The *Visalia Delta* of July 19, 1865, again vented its editorial rage, as well as reporting the murder at Jewett's ranch, and the subsequent rather easy escape of the perpetrators, moaning: "Mason and Henry Again. It is singular that these infernal scoundrels cannot be either captured, killed, or driven from the county; but go about robbing here, killing there, and intimidating in another place at their pleasure." There followed a series of probable crimes that Mason and Henry had committed, in addition to that at Jewett's Ranch: "It is believed that they robbed Mr. Eugene Calliard, merchant at Greenhorn, on the day before Johnson's murder."[39] The merchant barely escaped, indeed, from his store through a hail of bullets before the outlaws entered and plundered his mer.chandise.[40] The Indians at a rancho on the Kern River, near Jewett's sheep ranch, reported the dead body of a white man floating down the stream. The editorial went on to say that such affairs are a disgrace, and that settlers in the county were at the mercy of "murderous villains" who may depopulate a good part of the county unless captured.[41] The crimes named in the editorial may or may not have been the work of the former guerrillas, for the only available evidence is the *Delta's* accusation.

The *Delta* of July 19 also carried an article typical of the paper's War coverage: "It is stated that Jeff Davis walks his cell, and amuses himself by catching flies. That is fine sport for the miscreant traitor; possibly it is 'an evidence' of insanity or dementia."[42] Partisan feelings were apparently still strong on both sides.

Another "Mason and Henry Again" appeared in the *Delta* on August 23, 1865: "We are getting disgusted with chronicling the depredation of those two scamps, and begin to think that, if they can be secured neither by official nor private efforts, by military nor civilians, that the honest portion of the community had better sell out and give it (this valley) to Mason and Henry and the diggers [Indians]." The story of Mason and Henry depredations was continued, and it was alleged that, the previous week, Mason and Henry, or two of their band, came to McFarland's house in the Valley, just beyond Linn's Pass, ordered supper, and asked for the McFarland boys; after eating and drinking, the two robbed the man in charge of the house of what cash there was on hand, and charged the supper bill to Mason and Henry. It was surmised that the two were after the McFarlands, but no reason was given. A comment in the story was that, whilst they were eating, they left their loaded shotguns in another room. The editor did not tell how he knew the shotguns were loaded, but did offer a bit of thinly-masked criticism: "it does seem that a determined man might have secured the scamps. A show of following was made, as usual without effect." A bit of sarcasm concluded the article: "Probably, if the $2,500, now offered for their arrest, could be made available, they might be bought off to some other area."[43]

As it happened, it was not necessary to buy off Mason and Henry; the *Visalia Delta* of September 20, 1865, carried the headline, "Henry of the Mason and Henry Band of Thieves and Murderers Killed." The dispatch came by way of San Bernardino, dated September 18, from Los Angeles, dated September 16. The story was that Mason and Henry, with sixteen members of their band, had been in the mountains on the other side of San Bernardino, when they ran out of provisions and ammunition; Henry and John Rogers made the trip to purchase the needed items. Henry stopped about twenty-three miles from San Bernardino, and Rogers went on and made the purchases; having taken care of business, Rogers got drunk, and boasted that he was a member of the Mason and Henry band, was then arrested, and threatened with hanging, unless he would lead a posse to Henry's camp. When a noose was placed about his neck, be revealled the location of the camp, and that he was expected to meet Henry that night.[44]

As the *posse*, consisting of three soldiers and "two or three civilians,"[45] crept upon Henry's camp, a snapped twig alerted Henry, and he faced the *posse* with a six shooter in each hand. He received a hail of bullets, but managed to wound one of the *posse* in the leg before being shot down with "fifty-seven balls taking effect." From a *posse* of five or six men, and assuming that all shots fired by the *posse* hit Henry, the average number of shots fired by each member of the *posse* would have been approximately nine to eleven before Henry went down, unless, of course, Henry's dead body was shot up afterwards. The soldiers in the *posse* were, most likely, an element of Company K, Fourth California Infantry.

Henry's body was taken to San Bernardino, where it was photographed and identified by eight or nine men.[46] Many years later, it was disclosed that Mason, disguised as a woman, had come into town and viewed the body, the disposition of which is unknown; it was undoubtedly buried locally.[47] Rogers confessed the band had killed two men named Kimball and Williams on the Santa Ana River about two months earlier, and had been robbing and killing through that region. A party of citizens and a contingent of troops, probably also from Company K, Fourth California Infantry, started out after Mason and the other guerrillas.[48]

Seven months later, the death of Mason was reported. Under the title "Death of Mason," the *Delta* informed its readers it had "authentic information of the death of the desperado Mason." The story told was Mason had been killed by a *posse* of citizens at Tejon Canyon; two of his band, Tom Hawkins and West Overton, were reported to have been arrested at Clear Creek, and sent in irons to Los Angeles. It said also that thirty-five warrants for other members of the band had been issued.[49]

The capture of the men at Clear Creek, and the issue of thirty-five warrants, may well have been correct, but Mason did not die at the hands of a *posse* of citizens; the *Delta* of April 25, 1866, gave more accurate information. Mason had been in the habit of visiting the home of Jack McKinzie in the Tejon Canyon, and his visits seem to have involved a woman;[50] McKinzie was anxious to get rid of Mason, and the *Delta* reported he gave authorities information regarding Mason's whereabouts. Six men were said to have gone after Mason, "determined to capture or kill him, and, apparently preferring the latter, as Mason was considered to be entirely beyond the reach of human sympathy, and shut out by his terrible crimes from all claims to mercy." The men found "the wretch" in bed, and shot him there.[51]

An account of Mason's death, different from the two above described, appeared in the "Golden Century Edition" of the *Visalia Times Delta* of June 25, 1950; information had been taken from the old *Visalia Delta*, but a completely different version of Mason's death is given, in which two unnamed men had been traveling with Mason in September, 1866, although the *Delta* for April 25, 1866, had reported his death, and later admitted to murdering him, and burying him, "bed and all," saying nothing until the body was found.[52]

A fourth version is that Mason attempted to recruit a man named Ben Mayfield to join a new band after the death of Henry; Mayfield was not interested, and, fearing lest Mason should kill him, shot and killed Mason as he lay in bed. All versions agree that James Mason was shot whilst in bed.

The aftermath of Mason's murder seems quite indicative that the Mason and Henry organisation, by whatever name it was called, were considered by a significant number of people to have been a Confederate unit of resistance. Mayfield tried to hide Mason's body; being probably aware of the large number of secessionists in California, he was afraid a jury of Southern sympathisers would convict him of killing a Confederate guerrilla. He was correct. When the body was found, Mayfield was taken into custody, and tried at Los Angeles, "a city noted for her Southern sympathy during the late war," convicted, and sentenced to be hanged, but a flood of petitions caused his later acquittal. Mason's body is probably buried somewhere at an unknown location in Tejon Canyon.[53] The large number of warrants that had been issued earlier were already in the hands of officers; after Hawkins and Overton had been sent to Los Angeles, two fugitives were arrested at Elk Hill, of whom one was supposed to be Jack O'Brian, a member of the guerrilla band, but he gave his name as James Murphy. The other gave his name as Johnson. Murphy's appearance fit the description of O'Brian, but Johnson could not be identified with any wanted criminal; both, however, were sent to Los Angeles for identification.[54]

Tom Hawkins was hanged at Visalia in December, 1866, for his participation in the killing at the Kern River Sheep Ranch; the *Delta* reported he ascended the platform with firmness and composure.[55]

The man who founded and equipped the San Joaquin Valley Confederate guerrilla band, George Belt, was on business at Stockton on June 3, 1869, when he was shot and killed on the street by William Dennis, Belt's brother-in-law, who was convicted of murder, and died in prison;[56] Belt was apparently never charged with organising the guerrillas. John Gordon, the material supporter of the band, was also killed, in this instance by a former business partner.[57] The sympathy of the population of Kern County remained for the South during 1867, after the Military Reconstruction Act had been passed, and reconstruction by a Northern Army of Occupation was taking place; citizens of Kern County, joined by other

Californians of like sympathy, contributed money to the Southern Relief Fund. Those who served on the committee that had been formed at Havilah, a mining town founded by Asbury Harpending, included many prominent citizens; besides the solicitations, a money-raising festival was held at the Bella Union Hotel of Los Angeles, that had displayed a portrait of General Beaureguard in its lobby during the War. The proprietors, Henry Hammel and Andrew H. Denker, gave, free of cost, the use of the dining rooms and dancing saloon; the Secretary-Treasurer of the Kern County Southern Relief Committee reported more than $1,000 had been collected in there. A editor from Havilah wrote "well done" for the people of Kern County had "acted nobly in the manner of affording relief to the suffering people of the South."[58]

Those who have written about Mason and Henry generally refer to their band as the Mason and Henry Gang, and treat them as ordinary outlaws; one source even states that, after Belt had asked them to recruit a guerrilla band, they made an attempt in the Santa Clara and San Joaquin Valleys, and, failing in their effort, immediately abandoned their attempt at becoming guerrillas.[59] The *Visalia Delta*, nonetheless, in its editorial anger, provides good evidence that Mason and Henry were guerrillas, calling them "Democrats," "Peace Democrats," and "Constitutional Democrats," and speaking of them killing men for no other reason than that they were "Union men" who had voted for Lincoln in the election of November 8, 1864.

Even though the Mason and Henry Band were charged with crimes which had occurred a year or more before the organisation existed, and with other crimes which they may or may not have perpetrated, the first murders at their hands known for certain occurred during the 1864 presidential election, critical for supporters of Southern independence; the Union forces occupying Southern California were well aware of its potential for violence amongst those persons. Special Order N° 67, by command of Colonel Curtis, Headquarters of Southern California, dated November 5, 1864, was issued to prevent the kind of activity that began the assassinations perpetrated by Mason and Henry. The Special Order begins: "To preserve order, to ensure the loyal element in all of their privileges, and, as auxiliary to the civil authority of the county, detachments will proceed from Drum Barracks on the morning of the 6th instant, and will encamp during the presidential election of the 8th instant. …" The order describes the disposition of troops throughout Los Angeles County.[60]

Mason and Henry did what guerrillas do: kill the enemy, rob him of his sustenance, and live off the land. A guerrilla band cannot reasonably operate in an area that contains a majority hostile to their cause; it is thus very apparent that a majority of the San Joaquin Valley were sympathetic to the South, both before and after the War. Mason and Henry must have had sustained support from their "rebel friends" as charged by the *Delta*; they seem to have always had supplies, money, and fresh horses, which law officers and the army seemingly could not obtain at critical times, and even local law enforcement were suspected of cooperation with the guerrillas, and having friends amongst them.

People obviously knew Mason and Henry and their followers, but the reward for their capture did not attract much information, for, in Kern County, Union men were a beleaguered minority, and the Delta expressed a minority opinion, frequently attacking the general population of Visalia in reporting that Mason and Henry were receiving support.

From the autumn of 1864 until sometime during the summer of 1865, the Mason and Henry Band functioned as Confederate guerrillas; the *Delta* editorials seem to witness that they did. They did fight for the South and did engage Union troops in combat, such as the Second California Cavalry, Company E, from Camp Babbitt, and the Fourth California Infantry, Company K, from Camp Cady. There was little mention of plundering in the early days of the guerrilla's operation. The charges were mostly those of assassinations, as George Belt had ordered.

According to some sources the two may have split at the time of Henry's death, if so, Henry's men went to San Bernardino, and Mason's people remained in the valley near Tejon Canyon. The time of the split, in the summer of 1865, seems to have been the time when guerrilla activity ceased, and the former guerrillas became ordinary outlaws; neither Mason nor Henry were killed during a raid or in a gunfight typical of their time. Both, rather, were shot when it was impossible for them to defend themselves: they were ferocious, but brave men.

Though the deeds of Mason and Henry may seem similar to those of the many Confederate guerrilla bands in Missouri, they differed from those of Missouri in that they did not come from locally respected families, save Belt and Gordon. Both Mason and Henry were probably outlaws when they were recruited; however, they did follow the pattern of the James, Youngers, and Daltons in turning to crime when their cause was lost, and, in fact, they returned to outlawry.

There has been recent recognition of Southern guerrillas as Confederate veterans by such acts as the military funeral and burial of Jesse James, who was laid to rest on October 28, 1995, "in the soil he defended as a Confederate soldier." The Missouri Confederate battle flag was placed on his casket in the Memorial Chapel; his eulogy pointed out Jesse James and his family personified the suffering and sacrifice of 130 years before. The service was attended by the First Lady of Missouri and senior members of the state's General Assembly. The inscription on the grave gave the military affiliation of Jesse James:.

<blockquote style="text-align:center">
Taylor's Squad.
Todd's Company.
Quantill's Regiment.
C. S. A. [61]
</blockquote>

No such posthumous recognition is likely to be given Jesse's Californian comrades in arms, if their graves are ever found.

NOTES TO CHAPTER XI.

1. Jacks, James. "Civil War Changed the Lives of Kern Residents." *The Californian*. April 9, 1990. Civil War Clipping File. Local History Room. The Beal Memorial Library.
2. "Mason-Henry Outlaws Shielded by Civil War." *Visalia Times Delta*. "Golden Century Edition." June 25, 1959. Cols. 1-8.
3. Boyd, William Harland. *A California Middle Border: The Kern River Country, 1772-1880*. The Havilan Press. Richardson. 1972. p. 66.
4. Secrest, William B. *Lawmen & Desperados*. The Arthur Clark Company. Spokane. 1994. p. 175. and burial of Jesse James, who was laid to rest on October 28,
5. Secrest, p. 215.
6. Secrest, pp. 173-174.
7. Secrest, p. 215.
8. Jacks.
9. Secrest, p. 174.
10. Secrest, p. 215.
11. Secrest, p. 215.
12. Boyd, p. 66.
13. Secrest, p. 175.
14. *Visalia Delta*. April 25, 1866. p. 3. col. 2.
15. Berryhill, E. Richard. "Tulare County, Hotbed of Secession. 1861-1863." *Tulare County Historical Society Newsletter*. December, 1970. pp. 211-212.

16. Secrest, p. 216.
17. "$1,000 Reward." *Visalia Delta*. November 30, 1864. p. 2. col. l.
18. "Description of John Mason and McCauly, alias James Henry, The Murderer." *Visalia Delta*. November 30, 1864. p. 2. col. 1.
19. "Pursuit of the Peace Democrat Murderers, Mason and Henry." *Visalia Delta*. November 30, 1864. p. 2. col. 5.
20. "$500 Reward." *Visalia Delta*. November 30, 1864. p. 2. col. 2.
21. "Local News." *Visalia Delta*. December 21, 1864. p. 3. col. l.
22. Secrest, p. 175.
23. *Visalia Delta*. March 15, 1865. p. 3. col. 1.
24. *O. R.* Series I. Vol. L. Pt. 2. p. 1110.
25. *Visalia Delta*. March 15, 1865. p. 3. col. l.
26. "Telegraphic. Mason and Henry Heard From, Firebaugh Ferry, April 10." *Visalia Delta*. April 12, 186?. p. 3. col. 3.
27. Bowman, John S., Executive Ed. *The Civil War Almanac*. World Almanac Publications. New York. 1983. p. 268.
28. Davis, Jefferson. *The Rise and Fall of the Confederate Government*. Peter Smith. Gloucester.1971). p. 531.
29. Bowman, pp. 268-269.
30. Boyd, p. 65.
31. Bancroft, Hubert Howe. *The Works of Hubert Howe Bancroft*. Vol. VII. History of California, 1860-1890. The History Publishing Company. San Francisco. 1890. pp. 313.314.
32. *O. R.* Series I. Vol. L. Pt. 2. p. 1197.
33. *O. R.* Series I. Vol. L. Pt. 2. p. 1047.
34. *O. R.* Series I. Vol. L. Pt. 2. p. 1212.
35. *O. R.* Series I. Vol. L. Pt. 2. p. 1228.
36. Secrest, p. 217.
37. *Visalia Delta*. July 19, 1865. p. 3. col. 2.
38. Jacks.
39. *Visalia Delta*. July 19, 1865. p. 3. col. 1.
40. Boyd, p. 66.
41. *Visalia Delta*. July 19, 1865. p. 3. col. 1.
42. *Visalia Delta*. July 19, 1865. p. 3. col. 2.
43. *Visalia Delta*. August 23, 1865. p. 2. col. 1.
44. *Visalia Delta*. September 20, 1865. p. 2. col. 3.
45. Secrest, p. 176.
46. *Visalia Delta*. September 20, 1865. p. 2. col. 3.
47. Secrest, p. 176.

48. *Visalia Delta*. September 20, 1865. p. 2. col. 3.
49. *Visalia Delta*. April 18, 1866. p. 3. col. 1.
50. *Visalia Delta*. April 25, 1866. p. 3. col. 2.
51. *Visalia* Delta. April 25, 1866. p. 3. col. 2.
52. " ..... Outlaws Shielded by Civil War." pp. 1-8.
53. Secrest, pp. 217-218.
54. *Visalia Delta*. April 25, 1866. p. 3. col. 2.
55. *Visalia Delta*. June 25, 1959.
56. Secrest, p. 218.
57. Boyd, p. 67.
58. Boyd, pp. 66-67.
59. Secrest, p. 215.
60. *O. R.* Series I. Vol. L. Pt. 2. p. 1047.
61. Hawkins, Robert L. "A Confederate Funeral For Jesse James." *Confederate Veteran*. Vol. 3. 1996. pp. 50-54.

CHAPTER XII. EPILOGUE.

The most apparent conclusion which may be drawn is California was not passive during the War for Southern Independence; as in the nation as a whole, there were strong political and sectional feelings openly demonstrated throughout the state. California was a border state, if such a definition shall include the suppression of a portion of the press that was strongly sympathetic to the Southern cause, violence between civilians and the military, the necessity of stationing troops in some parts of the state for the purpose of maintaining order, volunteers from California fighting on both sides, and partisan and guerrilla warfare within the state: had California possessed a border contiguous with the declared states of the Confederacy, rather than a territory, she could well have been another Missouri.

A second conclusion, quite well documented, is that, even though a strong anti-administration, and often pro-Southern, minority were part of California's population, the majority of her people favoured the Union; the southern part of the state, especially Los Angeles, Fresno, Tulare, and San Bernardino Counties, had a Confederate majority, but those counties, though large in size, had a much smaller population than the northern part of the state. What is now called the Bay Area, around San Francisco, then contained most of the inhabitants, but, even so, there were constant Southern plots, hatched by pro-Confederate enclaves north of southern California, against the Union.

There was a great incompatibility between the two regions, and the state may well have split in twain before the War, had the timing of the election on that issue been different; the votes were there. A mob at San Francisco threatened a minister of the gospel, and drove him into exile, because of his Southern stance, and southern California elected state legislators who openly defied the Republican administration at Washington; it may be reasonably concluded Federal troops kept southern California from a liaison with the Southern Confederacy.

There is a strong indication that, had Confederate troops crossed the Colorado River into southern California, they would have been welcomed and supported by most of the population. The situation of a border state, like that of Kentucky or Missouri, would have resulted, and the effect of the war within California on the shipments of gold, so important to the North, is a significant question, as is the possible effect of an intrastate war on the war in general.

It is proper, if this line of thought is to be followed, to seek the reason why the Confederate thrust into California failed. The North possessed some obvious advantages; one is the fact that the United States Navy controlled the sea, for even the weak Pacific Squadron could not be matched by the Confederate Navy, and so a free-flowing line of supplies and men could reach California's ports from the eastern part of the Union. The overland path from the North taken by the Federal troops in their journey to California was unthreatened, and enabled the Colorado Volunteers to reinforce the defeated Union Army of the Southwest with ease in 1862. The Confederate Army's closest substantial base of supply was at San Antonio, more than a thousand miles of waterless desert east of California in Texas, and the Southern troops carried their irreplaceable lifeblood with them as they advanced to the west, which was destroyed by the Union cavalry when the opening afforded by General Sibley's neglect of his only stores and animals was exploited to the fullest.

In spite of the advantages held by the North, the Confederate armies under Baylor and Sibley won their battles, and brought combat to a point not 80 miles east of the Colorado River; mistakes were, however, made which cost the Confederate States their opportunity to provide the liberating army that southern Californians were praying would join them and establish their rallying point and strength for the casting off of the Union yoke.

Was California, with her ports, gold, and sympathetic population, especially in the southern part of the state, an important objective? The records of the Confederate government say that she was: but why, then, did Sibley turn north and east, towards Fort Union, by way of Apache Canyon and Glorieta Pass, rather than resume a westward thrust against little opposition? The only reasonable answer seems to be the necessity or the desire first to capture of the stores at Fort Union, but this failed deviation from the main objective destroyed all chance of Southern success in California.

The possibility of a Southern *coup d'etat* in 1861 failed when certain Californian secessionists believed erroneously that General Albert Sidney Johnston, the commanding officer of the Department of the Pacific, had less of a sense of honour than he did, and did not wait until Johnston and many of his officers had resigned their positions of trust in the United States Army in order to serve the South, after which the conspirators might have succeeded.

As the Union tightened her hold on California, the Democratic press came under constant attack by the Republican party; because a war was being fought under a sectional president, any disagreement with Republicans, in any form and even in the smallest degree, was regarded as treason. Many newspapers were considered pro-Confederate simply because they took the editorial position the Union, which they supported, had been split asunder by Lincoln and the abolitionists.

Most of the history of the War was written by Unionists who gave the Northern point of view; emotional words, such as "traitor," "desperado," "disloyal," "slavery me," "men of that stripe," and the like, are freely used; a review of events of the area of the War indicates tat most of the prominent supporters of the Confederacy in California were people of local prominence, who had been respected before the war, such as Albert Sidney Johnston, Joseph Lancaster Brent, Cameron Thom, Judge Daniel Terry, and Dan Showalter, who, albeit colourful, were hardly at the lower rungs of society. Terry and Showalter were not so different in their politics and personal lives from Andrew Jackson and other frontier politicians.

If it be taken into consideration that most North American Californians came from other cultures, and brought their social ways and politics with them into a single isolated state on the Pacific Coast, it is difficult to see why any one who claimed the South as his homeland, and was a Southern nationalist, would be a "traitor" or "disloyal" to northern states that he had never claimed as his own, yet, throughout the conflict within the state, those with allegiance to the South were denigrated and treated cruelly, in violation of the generally-accepted rules of war in the western world; prisoners of war were treated as criminals, tried in both civilian and military courts for treason, piracy, and violations of the criminal law, and denied recognition as prisoners of war.

Victors always write history, and so each succeeding generation is taught an history of California which is taken from primary sources written by those who fought to coerce the unwilling Southern states into a Union. California, at least northern California, would never have been a part of the Confederacy; such was not the will of the majority of her people, but the history of California would be more accurate and intriguing if the fierce struggle of a significant minority were, at last, to be universally acknowledged.

Laurence F. Talbott, PhD

INDEX OF NAMES.

Alvarados 30
Amyx, Fleming 58
Anderson, Ch. 140
Anderson, W. T. "Bloody Bill" 120
Armistead, Major L. 23, 25
Armistead, W. K. 23, 25
Ashman, Sh. J. S. 139, 140, 141
Baker, G. 123, 124, 126, 127, 130
Baker, Sen. T. 83, 85
Bancroft, H. H. .... xi, xii, 142
Baylor, Col. J. R. 23, 66, 80, 100, 101, 102, 154
Bean, Roy 31
Beaumont, Duncan 49, 66
Beaumont, H. 53, 66
Beauregard, Gen. P. G. T. 76
Bell, John 7
Belt, Geo. G. 122, 136, 137, 142, 147, 148, 149
Benbrook, Charles 63
Benjamin, Att'y Gen. J. P. 113
Bennett, Clarence E. 25
Biderman, J. W. ix
Bigler, Gov. John 74
Blake, Maj. G. A. H. 47
Bouldware, J. C. 126, 127, 130, 131
Boyd, Henry C. 115
Boyd, Wm. H. .... vii, 114, 136
Bragg, Gen. 128
Breckinridge, Vice-Pr. Jno. 7, 8
Brewer, William H. 74
Brent, Duncan K. 35
Brent, Gen. Jos. L. .... vii, 29, 30, 31, 32, 33, 34, 35, 39, 52, 76, 77, 94, 155
Brent, Nanine 35
Brent, Cong. Wm. L. 29
"Brigs, Esq." 47
Bright, John 114, 117
Brockway, Jdg. S. W. 129
Broderick, Sen. D. C. 44, 45, 46, 60
Brooks, Comptroller 92
Brown, D. W. 115
Browning, Sen. O. 14
Buchanan, Pres. James 3

Laurence F. Talbott, PhD

Buell, Maj. D. C. ... 47
Buonaparte, Napoleon ... 31
Burch, Cong. ... 69, 71

Calliard, Eugene ... 144
Calvert. Lord Geo. ... 29
Carleton. Col. J. H. ... 47, 48, 53, 61, 62, 64, 65, 80, 81
Carlisle, Roberts ... 19
Carillos ... 30
Carter, 1st. Lt. H. ... 64
Chapman, Deputy Sheriff ... 144
Cheatham, Gen. B. F. ... 92
Chivington, Maj. ... 105
Clendenning, J. ... 124, 126, 127, 130
Clendenning, W. ... 124, 126, 127, 130
Coit, Howard ... 34
Conness, Rep. Jno. ... 57
Conless, John ... 86
Crittenden, A. P. ... 30
Cross, George ... 124, 127
Crow, Alborn ... 115
Crowell, Henry ... 63
Curtis, Geo. T. ... ix, xii, 148
Curtis, Rep. ... 57
Curtis, L. C. J. F. ... 75

Dalton, Henry ... 30
Dalton, Kit ... 122
Daltons ... 149
Darg, Major ... 54
Davidson, Cap. J. W. ... 47
Davis, George W. ... 115
Davis, President Jefferson   11, 23, 32, 35, 47, 48, 49, 50, 51, 52, 53, 66, 75, 77, 81, 83, 90, 91, 92, 101, 111, 112, 113, 117, 120, 140, 141, 145
de la Peñas ... 30
del Valle, Ignacio ... 30, 31, 34
del Valle, Ysabel V. ... 34
Denker, Andrew H. ... 148
Dennis, William ... 147
Dominguez, Delores ... 76
Dominguez, Manual ... 29
Douglas, Steven ... 7, 8, 79, 82
Downey, Gv. J. G. ... 16, 19, 40, 69, 73, 76, 79, 81
Drum, Capt. R. C. ... 47, 122
Duval, Charles ... 47

Duval, R. H. 115
Dye, Joe 141

Edwards, William 63, 106
Evans, Col. 82, 83
Eyre, Maj. E. E. 61, 64

Ferguson, Maj. David 64
Field, Justice Stephen J. 54
Figueroas 30
Ford, Colonel John 65
Forman, Miss Anna 65, 66
Frears, James 124
Frears, Thomas 124
Fremont, John C. 7, 124
Fritz, Capt. Emil 64

Gamble, Joesph W. 124, 127
Garafias, Don Manuel 31
Garnett, Gen. Robert S. 92
Garrison, Samuel J. 82, 83, 85
Gately, John 124, 127
Gibson, Col. James 93
Gift, Lt. George W. 19, 34
Gill, Sheriff John 139
Gilllis, Maj. J. P. ix
Gilmore, Col. H. 121, 122
Glasby, A. H. 124, 125, 126, 127, 128, 129, 130
Glessel, Chapman & Smith 41
Gordon. John 137, 147, 149
Grant, Jim 124
Grant, Gen. U. S. 107, 142
Greathouse, R. 114, 115, 116
Greeley, Horace xii
Green, Frank 79
Green, Will S. 87
Griffin, Dr. J. 15, 18, 19, 77, 79
Griffins 11, 17, 30
Grover, James, L. 89
Gwin, Sen. W. M. 3, 4, 30, 32, 33, 34, 44, 74, 107

Hadley T. B. J. 43
Hall, L. P. 82
Halleck, Gen. Henry 120
Hamilton, H. 80
Harpending, A. 111, 112, 113, 114, 115, 116, 117, 123, 137, 148
Hastings, Jdg. L. W. 1, 43, 50, 51, 52, 53, 66

Hathwell, Belle 41
Hathwell, Susan Henrietta 39
Hawkins, T. 141, 144, 146, 147
Hawthorne, J. 138, 139, 140
Hays, Judge Benjamin 30
Hays, Col. Thomas 45, 60
Haythornthwaite, Phillip 121
Henderson, Capt. T. 47
Herbert, Congressman 92
Hindman, Gen. Thos. C. 120
Hitchcock, Dr. Charles 32
Hitchcock, Lillie 32
Hitchcock, M. H. 32
Hodges, P. 124, 125, 127, 130
Hughes, R. (Ran) 15, 19, 23, 25
Hunter, Capt. Sherod 106, 131
Hunter, Colonel 54

Ingram, John 123, 124, 127
Ingram, Capt. R. H. 75, 122, 123, 124, 125, 126, 127, 129, 130, 135, 137

Jackson, Pres. Andrew 1, 155
Jackson, Helen Hunt 31
James, Frank 120, 122
James, Jesse W. 120, 149, 150
Jarboe, Henry I. 124, 127
Jewett, Philo 144
Johnson, Pres. Andrew 41
Johnson, Judge James 128, 144, 147
Johnston, Gen. A. S.   11, 14, 15, 16, 17, 18, 19, 23, 25, 26, 30, 31, 35, 47, 49, 74,
    77, 113, 154, 155
Johnston. Gen. Jos. 128, 143
Johnston, Preston 15, 18
Jones, Lt. Col. Wm. 122, 135

Kennedy, Elijah R. xii
Kennedy, Capt. H. 66
Ketchem, Maj. W. S. 81
Kewen, Att'y. Gen. E. J. C. 78, 79
Kewen, Rep. E. J. C. 78, 79
King, Andrew 63, 79
Kirk, Major 54
Kreal, John 131

Lane, James Henry 120, 131
Laspeyre, Thomas 59
Latham, Sen. M. S. 3, 71

Law, William C. 115, 116, 117
Lee, Gen. R. E. .... ii, 54, 89, 90, 121, 128, 142, 143
Lee, Mrs. R. E. 89
Libby, Lorenzo 115, 116, 117
Lincoln, Pres. A. .... ii, 7, 8, 11, 14, 17, 33, 60, 71, 72, 73, 76, 77, 79, 82, 83, 86, 87, 90, 91, 93, 101, 107, 112, 117, 120, 138, 140, 141, 142, 143, 148, 155
Lincoln, Mary Todd 89
Loan, General 121
Loring, Col. William 100
L. A. Mtd. Rifles, Muster of the.. 20, 21, 22
Low, Gov. F. 115, 128, 138, 143

MacWillie, Cong. M. H. 50, 51
Magruder, Gen. J. B. 34, 53, 92
Mason and Henry 86, 122, 135, 136, 137, 138, 139, 140, 141, 142, 143, 145, 147, 148, 149
Mason, W. W. 115
Maximilian, Emperor 36, 107
Mayfield, Ben 147
Moore, William D. 115
Montgomery, Comm. J. B. 111
Morgan, E. M. 62
Mosby, Col. J. S. 121, 122
Munday, Capt. Patrick 143
McCauley, T. (Jas. Hy.) 136
McClellan, Gen. G. B.. .... 64, 79, 87, 92, 140, 141
McDowell, Gen. 107, 143
McFadden, J. W. 115
McLaughlan, Gen. M. 135
McMeans, Dr. 47

Neagle, U. S. Marshall 54
Nesmith, Sen. James W. 74
Noble, Capt. Herman 141

O'Brian, Jack, (*alias* Murphy) 147
Oldham, W. S. 51
Overton, West 146, 147
Owing, L. S. 99

Patrick, Capt. George L. 65
Pickett, John T. 111
Pickins, F. W. 23
Piercy, C. 57, 58, 59, 60, 62, 64
Pimientos 30
Poole, T. B. 115, 123, 126, 128, 129
Price, Gen. Sterling 35

Laurence F. Talbott, PhD

Quantrill, Wm. C. 120, 121, 123

Rains, John 19
Ranney, Constable G. 126
Reynolds, Maria 130
Rhodes, A. ix
Rhodes, Edward A. 88, 89
Rhodes, Mary 88, 89
Ridley, A. 19, 23, 25, 26, 34, 35, 36
Riley, General Bennet 2
Riley, Roger D. 88
Rigg, Maj. Edwin A. 47, 48, 62, 63, 64
Roberts, J. A. 53, 54
Roberts, T. L. 63
Robinson, E. G. 138, 140
Robinson, John A. 124, 127
Robinson, Mary C. 89
Rogers, S. A. 63
Rogers, Levi 63
Rogers, "Texas John" 141, 145, 146
Rollins, Major 81
Ross, Erskine 41
Rowley, Sargent 139
Rubery, Alfred 114, 115, 116, 117

Sayle, Judge 83
Scott, Congressman 69
Scott, Colonel H. L. 18
Scott, the Rev. Dr. W. A. 89, 90, 91, 92
Scott, Gen. Winfield 15, 18
Seddon, S'y of War J. A. 50, 52, 53
Seward, S'y of State W. 25, 33, 93, 141
Sexton, F. B. 51
Shannon, William E. 3
Sherman, Edwin 81
Sherman, Gen. Wm. T. 119
Showalter, D. .... iv, 47, 49, 54, 57, 58, 59, 60, 61, 62, 63, 64, 65, 66, 67, 80, 81, 82, 92, 93, 106, 155
Sibley, Gen. H. H. 60, 61, 101, 102, 105, 106, 154
Slaughter, Gen. J. E. 142
Smith, Col. George H. 41
Smith, Gen. E. K. 35, 50, 52, 53, 54, 66, 142
Stanford, Gov. L. 40, 71, 79, 81, 86
Staple, Const. Jos. 126, 129
Steele, Col. William 52

Stern, Abel 183
Stillman, Capt. Henry 65
Stroble, Serg. C. 85
Sumner, Gen. E. V. 17, 32, 33, 48, 73, 80, 81, 100
Swoup, Captain 54

Taylor, Gen. Richard 34
Taylor, Pres. Zachary 2, 14
Terry, Clinton 49
Terry, Judge D. S. 43, 44, 45, 46, 47, 48, 49, 50, 52, 53, 54, 60, 61, 66, 67, 93, 155
Terry, Mrs. David S. 49, 65
Terry, Frank 49
Terry, Jefferson Davis 49
Thom, C. E. 39, 40, 41, 94
Thomas, General L. 63
Tibbets, Jonathan 79
Todd, George 120
Totten, General James 120
Turner, William 63

Varella, Antonio 34, 35
Varella, Ysabel 31, 34
Verdugo, Don Julio 31

Walker, Gen. Charles J. 112
Ward, R. H. 63
Warner, J. J. 61
Washington, Geo. .... i, 87, 91
Watson, Dolores D. 76
Watson, Assemblyman J. A. 76, 77, 78, 79
Watson, R. E. Lee 79
Webster, Daniel 87
Weilman, 2nd. Lt. C. R. 62
Weller, C. L 74
Weller, Ex-Gov. J. B. 69
West, Lt. Col. J. R. 61
Wheeler, M. M. 143
Whidley, Judge 41
Wilcox, Jono A. 51
Williams (killed) 146
Willis, Henry M. 81
Wilson, Benjamin 76
Wilson, James 124
Wilson, T. A. 62, 63
Woodward, Arthur 58

Laurence F. Talbott, PhD

Wright, Gen. G. 62, 63, 64, 82, 83, 85, 93, 102
Wyllys, Rufus Kay 106
Younger, Cole 120, 122
Zamoranos 30

FINIS.

www.ingramcontent.com/pod-product-compliance
Lightning Source LLC
Chambersburg PA
CBHW070059080526
44586CB00013B/1128